Guide-book To The Industrial Exhibition

1851 Great Exhibition

GUIDE-BOOK TO THE INDUSTRIAL EXHIBITION.

One great object of the present work is, to furnish the visitor to the Exhibition, with some facts and figures, relative to the manufactures of our own and other countries; and to effect that, which the mere exhibition of specimens of raw material, or manufactured produce, fail to do, viz., to present a correct idea of the vastness and extent of that commercial enterprise so essentially the characteristic of the present day. The bundle of woollen, cotton, or linen yarn, and the bale of cloth, calico, or linen, may be passed unheeded by the visitor, who concentrates his admiration on the gorgeous display of gold and silver plate;—the block of coal, the pig of iron, or the bar of steel, may not attract a ten thousandth part of that attention which will be rivetted on the diamond of Koh-i-noor; but when the visitor is informed, that the annual value of the textile manufactures of our country, is not short of £95,000,000, the gold and silver plate sinks into comparative insignificance; and when he is reminded that the mineral products of our native land annually exceed in value £35,000,000, he will acknowledge, that the glittering gem of Golconda, is a feather in the scale, when weighed in the balance of utility, with the coal, the iron, and the other unprotected denizens of the western court of the Crystal Palace.

The exhibitions of art and industry, which, previous to the present year, have been opened in various manufacturing districts of our own country, such as Leeds, Manchester, and Birmingham, have been, for the most part, confined to the industrial products of the particular district. The last exhibition, at Birmingham, contained by far the best collection of the products of our manufactures that have been made in this country. Still, it was but a partial exhibition of our industrial resources, for although the varied manufactures of Birmingham itself were well illustrated, it must be remembered by all observant visitors, that the beautiful productions of the Coventry looms, in the same county, were anything but adequately represented. We do not therefore, consider it necessary to refer further to our own provincial exhibions, nor even to the triennial exhibitions at Dublin, eclipsed as they have been by those of Paris, Brussels, and Munich, preferring rather to occupy the brief space we can allot to the subject of previous exhibitions, with a succinct account of those, which, under successive dynasties, have served to advance the cause of national industry in France, and formed the proto-type of that universal exhibition, on which the attention of the whole civilized world is now centered.

Of the utility of exhibitions to the manufacturer, it will be almost unnecessary to speak. It is well known, that large orders were given to some Birmingham firms, on account of goods shown by them at the last exhibition; and, to say nothing of the large amount which is stated to be realized by Parisian and other French houses, as the produce of sales resulting from the exhibition of goods, at their quinquennial exhibition, one case in point may be mentioned, that of the house of Requillard & Co., carpet manufacturers, who, entirely from the publicity given to their products, at the Paris exhibition of 1849, disposed of carpets of the value of £10,000 to Russia alone.

FIRST EXHIBITION.—Although the Government of the day,—the Directory,—had previously collected together some of the finest specimens of French workmanship at the palace of St. Cloud, and thrown the collection open to public inspection, yet it was not until the 10th of September, 1798, that the first exhibition of French industry can be said to have taken place at Paris. That day was chosen as being the anniversary of the republic; this exhibition lasted but three days. The *locale* appropriated to the exhibition, was divided into 68 arcades, arranged in a square, having the temple of industry placed in the midst. The number of exhibitors were 110; twelve prizes were awarded, and certificates of honor granted to twelve other exhibitors.

SECOND EXHIBITION.—The second Exhibition was opened on the 19th of September, 1801, in the court-yard of the Louvre, under elegant porticos, and remained open seven days; 229 manufacturers exhibited the productions of their looms and workshops. At the close of the exhibition, Napoleon as first Consul, made a glowing address to the assembly, and recommended the adoption of an annual exhibition. Neither at this nor the former exhibition, was there any division of the productions exhibited, into classes, nor were the medals awarded with any classification; this did not take place until the third exhibition. On this occasion, Jacquard received a medal for the invention of the loom which bears his name.

THIRD EXHIBITION.—This exhibition was opened on the 19th of September, 1802, and, like the preceding one, lasted seven days. France was now at peace with England, and Fox, Erskine, and Lord Hawkesbury, were present at the exhibition; 540 persons exhibited the produce of their manufacturing industry. Specimens of soda made from sea salt were now for the first time exhibited, a discovery which has proved of immense importance to the industrial arts both of France and England,

FOURTH EXHIBITION was opened on the 25th day of September, 1806, and continued open for twenty-four days. The first Consul had now become Emperor of the French; during the four years which elapsed since the last exhibition, all the great industrial arts of the country had more fully developed themselves; the Merino sheep had been acclimatized, and the woollen manufacture become in consequence, much improved. The production of silk had received the greatest encouragement, and the looms of Lyons now sent out products, unequalled for their beauty and richness. Machinery had been applied to cotton manufactures,—the production of iron had increased,— and chemistry had lent powerful aid in developing new and important applications to the industrial arts. The number of exhibitors had increased to 1422.

FIFTH EXHIBITION. — The wars in which Napoleon was incessantly occupied, and the final occupation of the country by foreign troops, contributed to the postponement of the fifth exhibition to the year 1819. Louis XVIII, was now king of France; on the 25th of August, the exhibition was opened, and continued thirty-six days; the number of exhibitors amounted to 1662, of whom 17 were decorated with the Cross of the Legion of Honour, and 360 received medals of different kinds; the whole number of prizes awarded of every kind, amounted to 809.

SIXTH EXHIBITION.—This exhibibition, as well as the preceding one, took place in the palace of the Louvre, and was opened on the 25th of August, 1823. Charles X, was king of France. A slight diminution will be observed in the number of exhibitors, which, on this occasion, amounted to 1648. Since the last exhibition great progress had been made in the construction of improved machinery, especially for the use of the cotton manufacture. At this exhibition, a model of the first suspension-bridge erected in France, formed a leading object of attraction. The total number of medals, certificates of honour, &c., awarded at this exhibition, amounted to 1091; and although the number of exposants had diminished, yet the quality of the articles exhibited, had much improved.

SEVENTH EXHIBITION.—Was opened on the 1st of August, 1827. Considerable progress had now been made in the production of fine woollen cloths, merinos, cachemires, &c.; and this exhibition contained some fine specimens of the industrial resources of this branch of manufacture. The extended use of the cylinder in calico printing—the adaptation of the English methods of working iron, and the substitution of the rolling process for that of hammering; the application of steam to dyeing, distillation, and sugar refining; the employment of soda in the manufacture of glass; the introduction of lac dye, as a substitute for cochineal in dyeing; the manufacture of hydraulic cements; the improved method of manufacturing plate glass; and the restoration of the processes of painting and staining glass, were some of the leading characteristics of the exhibition of 1827. This exhibition was also held at the Louvre, and remained open fifty days. The number of exhibitors was 1795,—and 1,254 prizes, of various kinds, were awarded.

EIGHTH EXHIBITION.—Open from the 1st of May to the 1st of July, 1834. This exhibition, the first since the accession of Louis Philippe to the throne, greatly excelled those which preceded it. Four spacious pavilions were erected for the purpose, on the Place de la Concorde. The number of exhibitors had increased to 2,447, of whom 1,785 received favourable notice of the jury; 697 received medals; and 23 were decorated with the Cross of the Legion of Honour. M. Thènard, in his address to the King, stated, that no epoch had hitherto been so fertile in progress, and remarkable results. "It is especially in the last seven years," he said, "that French industry has advanced with rapid strides; our manufactories are multiplied, our machinery and manufactures improved, our commercial relations extended, and even new arts have sprung up amongst us." The following were amongst the objects for which medals were awarded, viz., improvements in sugar refining, dyeing, and the Jacquard loom; also for sulphuric acid, and other chemical products, and various mechanical improvements.

NINTH EXHIBITION.—The Great Square of the Champs Elysées, was now wisely selected as the site of the spacious building, destined to contain the specimens of the industrial progress of France, and the ninth exhibition was opened on the 1st of May, 1839, and, like the last, continued open two months. The number of exhibitors was 3,281; and 2,305 recompenses were awarded, of which 878 consisted of medals, of various kinds, and decorations of the Legion of Honour. Unmistakeable evidence was offered of the continued progress of the arts and manufactures generally. The following may be especially adverted to:—Chronometers, and public clocks; steam-engines; paper making machines; Jacquard looms; needles; galvanized iron; lithographic stones; decorated porcelain; muslins, silks, and shawls. It was also remarked, that whilst every branch of industry had advanced towards perfection, the price of its production had diminished.

TENTH EXHIBITION.—Opened on the 1st of May, 1844, and continued open 60 days. This was, undoubtedly, the "crack" exhibition, far surpassing all those which had preceded it, and, in many respects, even that of

1849; illustrating, in the most forcible manner, the great and important advantages which the industrial arts derive from the maintenance of peace and social order. Louis Phillippe was a constant visitor, accompanied generally by the Queen, and other members of the Royal Family. In addition to the splendid display of silks, shawls, woollen cloths, printed cottons, linens, laces, &c., a greater variety of novelties appeared on this than on any former occasion. It was on this occasion electro-plating was first exhibited, also the first locomotive-engines manufactured in France; a splendid collection of bronzes, carpets, tapestry, marqueterié, bijouterie ; optical, mathematical, and philosophical instruments, organs, harps, and pianos, contributed to show the beneficial results of a peaceful government on the industrial prosperity of the country. This exhibition, like the previous one, was held in the Champs Elysés; 3,960 persons exhibited the products of their skill, of whom 3,253 received the medals and certificates awarded by the jury.

ELEVENTH EXHIBITION.—The accidental overthrow of the Monarchy in 1848, and establishment of the Republic, was followed by such a commercial revolution, that the preparations for the exhibition of 1849, were commenced under circumstances of great depression. The exhibition was opened to the public on the 4th of June. The number of exhibitors was 4,494, being an increase of 534 over the number of the last exhibition. In metallurgy, machinery, chemical products, fine arts, and in all departments of woven goods, evident signs of progress and discovery were manifest. It was, indeed, no easy task for the jury to decide on the merits of the respective competitors, and we are not at all surprised to find that many, and in some cases, just complaints, were made against their decisions. The jury appointed to award the prizes at the Great Exhibition of 1851, will have a most unthankful as well as most difficult task to perform, and we are inclined to think that it will be far better to omit altogether the distribution of medals, and leave the question of reward to the discernment of the public, who will convey their approbation in terms more durable and lasting than a bronze medal. The exhibition remained open eight weeks, being four days short of the period allowed at the exhibitions of 1844 and 1839. The number of prizes of all kinds awarded to the exhibitors was 1671, of these 52 were Crosses of the Legion of Honour, 182 gold medals, 540 silver medals, and 897 bronze medals. The building for this exhibition was 675 feet long by 328 wide, exclusive of the space for the agricultural department, and covered an area of 240,000 square feet, about one-third the area of the Crystal Palace. Around the four sides of the building extended a gallery about 90 feet wide, divided into two avenues by a double range of pilasters; the whole width of gallery was so arranged that there were four passages for visitors, two rows of manufactured goods on stalls, two rows placed against walls, and one row between and around the pilasters. The interior area of the great quadrangle was crossed by two transverse galleries, which thus left three courts, one of which contained a beautiful fountain and a horticultural collection; another had an immense reservoir; and the third contained specimens of large metal work. In addition to the main building was a shed of large dimensions, about 300 feet long by 100 in width, appropriated to the reception of agricultural implements and live stock; for it was one peculiar feature of this exhibition, as compared with its predecessors, that the skill of the grazier was represented as well as that of the manufacturer. The entire range of buildings was constructed of wood, and roofed with zinc; the cost was about £16,000; the materials becoming the property of the contractors after the conclusion of the exhibition. The exhibition was open to the public four days in each week; on Thursdays the price of admission was one franc, the proceeds of which were devoted to the public hospitals of Paris; and Mondays was especially devoted to the juries. The expenses of the building, and of the carriage of all articles sent for exhibition from the departments were, as hitherto, defrayed by the Government.

THE CRYSTAL PALACE.

WE now proceed to give a few particulars relative to the origin and construction of the "Crystal Palace of Industry."

This industrial palace of glass, iron, and wood, is remarkable, not only as a new design, but for the wonderful rapidity of its construction, and the immense resources of manufacturing power, and manual skill, employed upon it. The plans sent in to the Royal Commissioners for the building, were 229 in number; of these designs, 34 were contributed by foreigners, 128 by residents in London and its environs, 50 by residents in provincial towns in England; 6 by residents in Scotland; 3 by residents in Ireland; and 7 anonymous. Possession of the site, in Hyde-park, was obtained July 30, 1850, but when the various plans were laid before the Commissioners, none were found perfectly adapted to the purpose required; and many forcible objections were raised to the erection of any building of bricks and mortar in Hyde-park; besides which, it would have been impossible to get the walls of such a building *dry* in time. Amongst the forcing-houses and conservatories of Chatsworth and Darley-Dale, the genius and scientific skill of Mr. Paxton had for years been continually introducing improvements, until at last, the nearest approach to perfection, in glass erections, had been shown to the world, in the renowned Victoria Regia-house, built at Chatsworth, in 1849. Thus, no sooner did Mr. Paxton turn his attention to the subject of the exhibition, than he was ready, not only with the idea of a suitable building, but was prepared with proof of its practicability; and the Victoria Lily-house served as a model, in its principles and modes of construction.

The fitness of this design for an industrial exhibition, its suitableness to the site intended, and its capability of permanence, if required, at once commended it to the choice of the commissioners; and the late Sir Robert Peel greatly approved the general features of the building. Neither stone, brick, mortar, or any moist material is used, but a combination of iron, wood, and glass, rendering this the dryest, as well as the lightest building, which could have been provided. The dimensions of the building are 1,851 feet in length, or four times the length of St. Paul's, and 456 feet in breadth in the widest part. The height of the centre isle is 64 feet; the transept is 108 feet in height, and is covered with a semi-circular roof, in order to preserve and enclose the large elm trees opposite Prince's-gate. The building covers more than eighteen acres of ground, and the whole is supported upon 3,300 cast-iron pillars or columns, united by bolts and nuts, fixed to flanges turned perfectly true, and resting on concrete foundations. There are 2,224 cast and wrought-iron girders. The smelting and casting were performed at the iron works of Messrs. Cochrane and Co., near Dudley, and the London works of Messrs. Fox and Henderson, at Smethwick, in Staffordshire.

There are three large refreshment courts, and on each side of the central aisle, and at both ends of the buildings, are places for paying, committee-rooms, apartments for the commissioners, clerks, &c. Four longitudinal galleries, 24 feet wide, run the whole length of the building, and there are six transverse ones of the same dimensions: these galleries are suited for the display of light manufactured goods; and will afford a complete view of the interior of the building, and the articles exhibited in it. In order to give the roof a light and graceful appearance, the whole of it, including the semi-circular transept, is built on the ridge and furrow principle, and glazed with British sheet glass, made by Messrs. Chance and Co., Birmingham, the sheets being 49 inches long. The quantity of glass used in the building is about 1,200,000 square feet, and the weight of it 400 tons. The rafters are inclined in uninterrupted lines, the whole length of the building. Some years since, Mr. Paxton had invented an apparatus for forming sash-bars, and all the upright sashes, used in the building, as well as the roof, being made by machinery, and fitted and finished before they were brought, on the ground, were put together and glazed with great rapidity. The length of sash-bar used is 205 miles. The lower tier of the building is, however, enclosed in boarding. The glazing was performed with great rapidity, each man fixing on an average, 200 superficial feet of glass per day. To save time in glazing the transept, one of the foremen at the works contrived an ingenious apparatus, a sort of moveable platform, each capable of mounting eight glaziers, who were hauled up or down, or sideways, as their work required, and by the use of numbers of these machines, pane after pane was fixed without any delay. The gutters are arranged longitudinally and transversely. The rain-water passes from the longitudinal gutter, into a transverse gutter over the girders, and is thus conveyed to the hollow columns, and thence to the drains below. As these transverse gutters are placed at every 24 feet apart, and as there is a fall in the longitudinal gutters both ways, the water has only to run a distance of 12 feet, before it descends into the transverse gutters, which carry it off to the hollow columns, or down pipes. The grooves for carrying off the moisture which condenses on the inside of the glass, are cut out of the solid; in fact, the whole gutter is formed by machinery at one cut. The flooring of the industrial building was an important point; here again, Mr. Paxton's experience in horticultural structures, suggested the adoption of that method of flooring, which, for those purposes has been found to answer best, viz: trellised wooden paths. In the exhibition building, the boards of the floor are 9 inches broad, and 1½ inch thick, laid half-an-inch apart, on sleeper joists, 9 inches deep, and 3 inches thick, placed 4 feet apart. Before sweeping the floors, the whole will be sprinkled with water from a moveable hand-engine, which will be immediately followed by a sweeping machine, consisting of many brooms, fixed to an apparatus on light wheels, and drawn by a shaft. This method of flooring is economical, dry, clean, and pleasant to walk upon. The galleries are laid with close boardings. The ventilation of the building has been carefully considered, and a copious supply of fresh air has been provided for. Four feet round the whole of the basement part of the building is made of *louvre-boarding*, which is simple in construction, and can by simple machinery be instantaneously opened and closed. At the top of each tier a similar provision of 3 feet is made, with power to add an additional quantity if required; at the same time the arrangement of the *louvre-boards* effectually prevents the entrance of wet in rainy weather. In the centre aisle also, the air will be plentifully admitted.

A provision is also made for the Indian method of ventilation, if the heat should be so intense as to render it desirable to have the temperature lower than out of doors.

In order to subdue the intense light, all the south side of the upright parts of the building, and the whole of the angled roof, is covered outside with unbleached calico, so fixed as to allow a current of air to pass between the canvas and the roof. In very hot weather, water may be poured on, to cool the interior. By this covering the glass will also be protected from injury by hail. In the interior, magnifying glasses, working on swivels, will be placed at short distances, to give additional facility for commanding a perfect general view of the exhibition. No apprehension need to be entertained as to the strength and security of the galleries, for assuming that their whole surface could be covered with a dense crowd (which it could, not), the pressure would be about 112 lbs. per superficial foot, or a load upon each girder of about $5\frac{1}{4}$ tons. These girders have been proved to 15 tons, and will not break under a pressure of 30 tons. On each side of the exit doors, of which there are about twenty, there are glass windows, so that in the event of fire occurring at any part, it could at once be seen, and extinguished. For the supply of water, an ample provision is made, by the Chelsea Water-Works Company; and a special engine provided, able to supply 300,000 gallons per day. As to storms, a heavy gale was sustained, without any injury, while the building was in progress, and before the diagonal gallery-flooring, or roof, were complete, and the same thickness of glass has been used, in various buildings, by Messrs. Fox, and Henderson for years; amongst other places, at Woolwick dockyard. The construction of the building also provides for the effects of contraction and expansion, consequent on changes of temperature.

Messrs. Fox and Henderson are the contractors, and Mr. Fox has personally superintended the erection from the time of its commencement. The general management was entrusted to Mr. Cochrane. The setting out of the ground was managed by Mr. Brownger; the contrivance of the machines by Mr. E. A. Cooper; and the raising of the arches by Mr. Wilbee.

The amount of the contract by Messrs. Fox and Henderson, for the use and waste of the materials employed in the building, is £79,800, the whole building to become the property of the contractors, and to be removed by them. If, on the contrary, the building be permanently retained, the cost will be £150,000.

ARRANGEMENT OF THE EXHIBITION.

The leading feature of the arrangement of the Exhibition is, that the ground floor and the galleries, to the west of the transept, is allotted to the productions of Great Britain and her colonies, the part east of the transept being assigned to foreign countries. The transept galleries are devoted to the display of British goods. As far as possible, some attention has been paid to latidude in the position assigned to each foreign country, and to the colonies. On the foreign side of the transept, each nation has arranged its productions, according to its own taste. On the British side, a particular locality has been assigned to each of the thirty sections, into which British productions have been divided, the arrangement of the articles of each exhibitor being made according to his own plan. The lighter articles are placed in the galleries, and the heavy on the ground As any general direction to proceed from one part to the other would be of no service to the visitor, certain sections, exciting the interest of one, to which another would be indifferent, we propose to give an account of the various objects exhibited under each section, and to point out its situation; with this guide, the visitor, on entering the building, can direct his steps to the objects of most interest to him, without loss of time.

* SECTION 1.—*Raw Materials.*—*Mining, Quarrying, Metallurgical Operations, and Mineral Products.*—This section contains some remarkable specimens of iron, copper, and other ores and metals, in an unmanufactured state. The splendid specimens of the native "black diamond" here exhibited, will be regarded with much interest, when it is remembered how much we are indebted to our abundant supply of coal, for the success of our manufacturing operations. The specimens of other raw materials used in the arts and manufactures, are deserving of attention.—*See* p. 20.

SECTION 2.—*Chemical and Pharmaceutical Processes and Products generally.*—The successful operations of manufacturing chemistry, are illustrated in the varied specimens of crystalline and other products exhibited, and of pigments and colours employed in various manufactures. The rarer chemical substances, manufactured for the use of the scientific chemist

---

* We employ the term "section," instead of class, as the former name has been adopted (and we think correctly) in the classification of the Head Juries.

will here be found; also the various chemical and pharmaceutical substances derived from the mineral, vegetable, and animal kingdoms, used in medicine and pharmacy.—*See* p. 25.

SECTION 3.—*Substances used as Food.*—In this department will be found specimens of all kinds of agriculture and other produce; for more particular information upon which subject, we refer the reader to pp. 49, 50.

SECTION 4.—*Vegetable and Animal Substances, chiefly used in Manufactures as Implements, or for Ornaments.*—Of most of the leading articles exhibited in this section, as cotton, flax, wool, silk, &c., a particular account will be found under the heads of the various manufactures to which they relate.

SECTION 5.—*Machines for direct use, including Carriages and Railway and Naval Mechanism.*—The splendid array of steam engines, locomotives, railway carriages, and machinery, forming the chief features in this extensive section, will serve to give the visitor some idea of that immense development of steam power, which has produced such a revolution in our mode of travelling, and by the increased facility afforded to commercial transit, so greatly promoted the prosperity of trade.

The hydraulic machinery employed in the construction of the Britannia Bridge, will be viewed with much interest; the superb collection of carriages adapted for travelling and general use, incontestably proves our superiority in this branch of manufacture.—*See* pp. 52, 59 61, 62, 63, 164.

SECTION 6.—*Manufacturing Machines and Tools, or Systems of Machinery; Tools and Implements employed for the undermentioned purposes, viz:*—Machinery employed in the manufacture of cotton, wool, flax, hemp, silk, and other fabrics, in paper-making, printing, and book-binding; in the manufacture of metals from the ore into bars, rods, wires, sheets, and other general forms; also in the preparation and working of various mineral, vegetable, and animal substances, such as glass, wood, stone, bone, ivory, leather, &c. The various tools used in the manufacture of machinery are exhibited in this section, together with mills and machines for grinding, crushing, or preparing vegetable products; also machinery and apparatus used for brewing, distilling, and manufacturing chemistry.—*See p.* 85. 164.

SECTION 7.—*Civil Engineering; Architectural and Building Contrivances.*—The wide field embraced by this section, comprehends, foundations and building contrivances, connected with hydraulic works; scaffoldings, centerings, bridges, and tunnels; dock, harbour, river, and canal works; lighthouses and beacons; roofs and buildings; water and gas works; contrivances connected with the sanitary condition of towns; warming and ventilating of domestic residences, and other miscellaneous contrivances.—*See p.* 71.

Section 8.—*Naval Architecture, Military Engineering, Ordnance Armour and accoutrements.*—Including models of vessels, for purposes of war and commerce; rigging, anchors, windlasses, &c.; and articles connected with practical seamanship, and the saving of life from shipwreck and naval gunnery, artillery, equipments, arms of various kinds, ordnance and projectiles, together with army clothing, and accoutrements, &c.

Section 9.—*Agricultural and Horticultural Machines and Implements.*—The extensive collection of machines and implements, forming a complete exhibition of itself, represents the annual show of the Royal Agricultural Society; and comprises the various implements for tillage; also drilling, sowing, manuring, and harvesting machines; the machinery of the barn and farm yard; agricultural carriages, harness, and gear; implements for draining, and machines for making pipes, tiles, and bricks; dairy utensils, and the miscellaneous machines and implements used in agriculture.—*See p. 51.*

Section 10.—*Philosophical Instruments, and processes depending upon their use.—Musical, Horological, and Surgical Implements.*—In this section are comprised telescopes, microscopes, barometers, thermometers, areometers, scales, balances, nautical instruments, and various others employed to illustrate the laws of mechanics, optics, light, heat, and electricity; also chemical and pharmaceutical apparatus generally. The department of musical instruments presents an immense and most attractive variety. In addition to the electric-clock, placed over the principal entrance to the building, the horological department of this section will be found to contain a large assortment of clocks, chronometers, watches, &c., with various portions of mechanism, forming parts of, or applicable to them. The department of surgical instruments will be chiefly interesting to the members of the medical profession.—*See pp. 41, 64 to 75.*

Section 11.—*Cotton Manufacture.*—Of this important branch of the manufactures of our country, some account will be found in a subsequent portion of the work; it is here represented by yarn and thread; calicoes, sheetings, and shirtings; cambrics, jaquenots, and figured muslins; velvets and velveteens; shawls, handkerchiefs, and muslin dresses; plain and figured dimities; ginghams, and coloured cotton handkerchiefs, &c., the productions of Manchester, Glasgow, Paisley, and other manufacturing towns.—*See p. 112.*

Section 12.—*Woollen and Worsted Manufacture.*—The broad and narrow cloths of Gloucestershire, Wiltshire, and Yorkshire; the flannels of Rochdale and Wales; the blankets of Witney and Dewsbury; the woollen cloaking, serges, and stuff goods, of Leeds, Halifax, and Huddersfield; and the tartans of Paisley, are here well represented by the varied specimens exhibited in this section.—*See p. 97.*

Section 13.—*Silk and Velvet Manufacture.*—This section contains the most showy specimens in the department of textile fabrics. The gorgeous array of plain and fancy silks, and plain and figured velvets, will rivet the attention of the visitor, and will perhaps elicit, more than in any other class of goods, a comparison with the productions of the French loom. The exhibition of ribbons from Coventry, will bear comparison with those of St. Etienne and St. Chamond, and the contents of the Spitalfields trophy in the nave of the building will not yield the palm of excellence to the silks and velvets of Lyons.—*See* p. 107.

Section 14.—*Manufactures from Flax and Hemp.*—In addition to plain linen yarn and thread, this section contains specimens of canvas, heavy linens, Irish linens and sheetings, plain linens of all widths, bleached, unbleached, and dyed; also damasks, diapers, drills, twilled linens, linen velveteens, velvets and cords; and also specimens of cambrics, cambric and linen handkerchiefs, printed linens, lawns, &c., and, by way of contrast, cordage of all kinds, ropes, lines, twines, nets, &c.—*See* p. 118.

Section 15.—*Mixed Fabrics, including Shawls, but exclusive of Worsted Goods.*—This section is devoted to various mixed woven fabrics, in which the warp is either of cotton, silk, or linen, and the shoot of wool, mohair, linen, silk, silk and cotton, or worsted, or China grass, constituting what are termed tabinets, poplins, challis, baréges, paramattas, tweeds, plaids, and other materials for articles of dress or furniture. The splendid assortment of shawls, in this section, show the great progress which has of late years been made in this manufacture.—*See* p. 132.

Section 16.—*Leather, including Saddlery and Harness, Skins, Furs, Feathers, and Hair.*—Among the varied contents of this section may be enumerated, specimens of rough tanned and curried leather, of various kinds; black and coloured enamelled and dyed leather, for bookbinding and other purposes; buckskin, doeskin, and other specimens of oiled leather; white or alum leather for gloves, and ladies' shoes; sheep and other skins for rugs; with parchment and vellum for deeds, bookbinding, drum-heads, &c. The collection of saddlery and harness, shows our marked superiority over other countries in this respect. The splendid collection of skins and furs, for ladies' apparel, army clothing, accoutrements, and other purposes, cannot be surpassed. This part of the section, and that of feathers, will prove very attractive to the ladies. Nor must the last department be overlooked, viz., hair, presented in the varied forms of utility and ornament.—*See* p. 137.

Section 17.—*Paper and Stationery; Printing and Bookbinding.*—Here may be seen paper in the raw state, as it leaves the mill, and in every description of ornamental and useful forms. Pens, ink, wafers, wax, are also included; with cards, cardboard, pasteboard, and paper and cardboard boxes and cases of all kinds. Printing inks and varnishes; and type printing generally; together with the various kinds of bookbinding, in cloth, leather, velvet, &c., are included in this section.

SECTION 18.—*Woven, Spun, Felted, and Laid Fabrics, shown as Specimens of Printing or Dyeing.*—This section comprises specimens of woollen, silk, cotton, and mixed fabrics, which are shown in this department, without reference to the materials of which they are composed, expressly to exhibit the processes of dyeing and printing.—*See* p. 136.

SECTION 19.—*Tapestry, including Carpets and Floor-cloths, Lace, Embroidery, Fancy and Industrial Work.*—The extensive series of articles comprehended in this section, cannot fail to attract considerable attention, as it includes some of the finest specimens in carpets, lace, and fancy work, which have ever been produced in this country. The carpets exhibited vie with those of France. Here are specimens of pillow lace, made wholly by hand; of bobbin-net, tulles, blondes, &c., made wholly by machinery; and of lace, the ornamental part of which is made by hand, and the ground by machinery. All kinds of embroidery and fancy work are included in this section.—*See* pp. 123, 129.

SECTION 20.—*Articles of Clothing, for immediate Personal or Domestic use.*—In this section are classed hats, caps, and bonnets; hosiery and gloves of all kinds; also, boots and shoes, and upper and under-clothing in general.—*See* pp. 123, 129.

SECTION 21.—*Cutlery and Edge Tools.*—The varied assortment of knives of all kinds, for the table and the pocket, office knives, and knives used in various trades; forks, scissors, shears, razors, and other miscellaneous articles, are included in this section; also files and other small edge tools, not included under manufacturing tools, in section 6: such as the files and edge tools used by engineers and smiths, for building purposes, for fine metal and other work; carpenters tools, &c.; together with drawing and engraving instruments.—*See* pp. 148 to 157.

SECTION 22.—*Iron and General Hardware.*—This, which may be termed the Birmingham section of the exhibition, comprises articles of brass, iron, copper, zinc, tin, and pewter manufacture; such as metallic bedsteads, stoves, grates, fenders, fire-irons, cooking and warming apparatus, kettles, coal-scuttles, saucepans, and an immense variety of articles for domestic use; also pewter, german silver, and britannia metal teapots, spoons, and forks, chandeliers, lamps, and candlebra, gas fittings, metallic tubing of all kinds, garden implements, iron safes, cash boxes, nails, screws, bolts, and general ironmongery; also articles of steel manufacture, such as hammers, vices, steel ornaments, pens, needles, fish-hooks, and fishing-tackle. This section also contains every variety of buttons, whether of metal, bone, pearl, &c.; also wire-work of all kinds, whether of iron, brass, steel, or copper, pins, hooks and eyes, wire baskets, and wire rope.—*See* pp. 38, 42, &c., 76, &c., 157, &c.

SECTION 23.—*Working in precious Metals, and their Imitations; Jewellery and all articles of Vertu and Lapidary work, not included in any previous Section.*

We now come to the gorgeous display of gold and silver plate, communion services, and gold and silver articles applied to decorative purposes, presentation pieces, &c.; also the smaller articles of plate in domestic use, whether for the breakfast, tea, or dinner table; also chains, seals, keys, and other miscellaneous articles. In this section are included electro-plated goods of all descriptions, comprehending all that can be executed in silver or other metals; also Sheffield and other plated goods of all kinds; gilt and or molu work; jewellery of all kinds, as works exhibiting the precious stones and pearls, and the manner of setting them; plain and enamelled ornaments of gold, as bracelets, brooches, &c.; jewellery by imitations of precious and other stones; and ornaments worked in jet, ivory, horn, hair, and other materials. In this section are also included ornaments and toys, worked in iron and steel, such as chatelanes, chains, Berlin iron ornaments, &c.; also enamelling and damascene work; and various other metallic articles of use, ornament, and curiosity.—*See* pp. 24, 144.

SECTION 24.—*Glass.*—In addition to the specimen furnished by the building itself, the space alloted to this section contains illustrations of the various processes used in manufacturing glass, and includes specimens of sheet glass, crown glass, coloured and silvered sheet glass, glass shades, ventilators, painted, enamelled, embossed, and ornamented window glass: also plate glass, bottle glass, bottles of various kinds, water pipes, and tubing; glass for chemical, optical, and philosophical apparatus, &c. The splendid assortment of flint or crystal glass, in the varied forms of chandeliers, table vases, glasses, decanters, &c., of coloured, encrusted, enamelled, and silvered glass, present a magnificent display.—*See* p. 91.

SECTION 25.—*Ceramic Manufacture, Porcelain, Earthenware, &c.*—This interesting section contains illustrations of every branch of the ceramic art; from the common garden flower-pots, to the finest and most delicate specimens of English porcelain. Here are specimens of glazed and unglazed stone-ware, of various kinds of earthenware in common use; of hard and tender porcelain; terra cotta ornaments; encaustic tiles and tesseræ; bricks, tiles, &c. The beautiful specimens of statuary porcelain—a manufacture of recent date—will deservedly attract especial notice.—*See* p. 87.

SECTION 26.—*Furniture and Upholstery, including Paperhangings, Papier Maché, and Japanned Goods.*—The space allotted to this section is replete with the productions of the decorative arts: and is rich in inlaid, carved, and ornamental cabinet work. The ecclesiastical edifice fitted up by Messrs. Pugin, Crace, Hardman, Minton, and Myers, will prove a source of considerable attraction. The beautiful papier maché and japanned goods, inlaid with pearl and tortoiseshell, join with the elegant display of paperhangings, in making this one of the most generally attractive in the exhibition.

SECTION 27.—*Manufactures in Mineral Substances, used for Building or Decorations, as in Marble, Slate, Porphyries, Cements, Artificial Stones, &c.*—This section includes manufactures in common stone, for building and decorative purposes; in marble, alabaster, and Derbyshire spar, for useful and ornamental purposes, as chimney-pieces, articles of furniture, tables, &c.; also manufactures in slate, cement, and artificial stone; specimens of inlaid work in stone, marble, and other mineral substances; ornamental work in plaster, composition, scagliola, and imitation marble.—p.166.

SECTION 28.—*Manufactures from Animal and Vegetable Substances, not being Woven, Felted, or included in other Sections.*—A great portion of this section is occupied by the various articles manufactured from caoutchouc or india-rubber, forming a great variety of waterproof and elastic articles; and the manufactures from gutta-percha, comprising specimens of its adaptation to waterproofing purposes, decorative uses, ornamental mouldings, picture frames, &c., for maritime purposes and agricultural uses. There are also exhibited articles exemplifying its use for surgical, electrical, and chemical purposes, as well as to domestic and miscellaneous uses, as the lining of cisterns, gas and water-pipes, &c. This section also includes manufactures from ivory, tortoiseshell, bone, horn, bristles, and vegetable ivory; also specimens of wood turning and carving, cooper's work, basket and wicker work; also manufactures from straw and grass, and sundry manufactures from animal and vegetable substances.—*See* pp. 139 to 143.

SECTION 29.—*Miscellaneous Manufacture and Small Wares.*—In this section will be found perfumery and soap; articles for personal use, as writing desks, dressing cases, workboxes, and travelling necessaries. Another department of this section is occupied with artificial flowers; another with candles, &c.; whilst confectionary, of all kinds, also finds a place in this section. Beads, toys, fans, umbrellas, parasols, walking-sticks, fishing-tackle, archery, and miscellaneous articles, complete the list of sundries exhibited in this section.—*See* pp. 28, 29, 131.

SECTION 30.—*Sculpture, Models, and Plastic Art.*—This last section is devoted to specimens of sculpture in gold, silver, bronze, iron, and metallic substances; in marble, porcelain, wood, ivory, &c. It also includes works in die-sinking, intaglios, medals, gems, &c.; mosaic and inlaid work, and enamels; lithography, zincography, ornamental printing, encaustic painting, and lastly, models in architecture, topograpy, and anatomy.—*See* pp. 161,163.

POSITION OF SECTIONS NUMBER OF EXHIBITORS, AND SPACE ALLOTTED

Sect.	No. of exhibtrs.	Feet of ground.	Feet of wall.	Low. bays.	Upper bays.	Position.
1	353	8881	2343	46	—	Extreme south ground floor and W. court
2	166	1776	505	—	6	South gallery.
3	171	2443	3560	—	8	Ditto.
4	193	3343	2075	—	11	Ditto.
5	553	29700	2600	89	—	Inner division of northern ground floor.
6	326	34300	2580	103	—	Outer ditto. ditto.
7	195	6000	2182	—	18	North gallery.
8	331	6000	2190	18	—	Central south gallery.
9	—	25000	—	—	—	South ground floor.
10	515	7400	3705	—	23	North central and south cent. galleries.
11	73	1535	5640	6	—	North central ground floor.
12	125	4749	16100	15	—	South ditto.
13	95	1212	2807	—	6	Transept gallery, S. W.
14	102	3784	13844	—	12	South central ground floor.
15	80	3799	8004	15	6	Ditto ditto.
16	186	2321	5494	5	—	North central ditto.
17	170	1353	2987	11	—	Ditto ditto.
18	98	2146	12489	—	8	South central ditto.
19	266	2440	51800	—	10	North gallery.
20	220	8526	3566	—	8	Transept gallery, S. E.
21	60	3441	557	—	12	N. cent. gallery and S. cent. grand floor.
22	798	18404	8865	32	8	South central ground floor.
23	120	9405	233	—	18	South central gallery.
24	50	2531	5727	—	9	North central gallery.
25	80	4313	3583	—	14	Transept gallery N. W.
26	368	10638	20567	25	—	North and south central grand floor.
27	98	3841	1699	—	—	North central ditto.
28	170	1482	2212	—	—	North gallery.
29	358	1991	1258	—	7	Transept gallery N
30	—	10716	5470	—	11	Transept, nave, and Fine Art court.

MINERAL PRODUCTS—MANUFACTURE OF IRON.

Produits Mineraux—Berg Producte.

We feel that we cannot do better than commence our notices of the manufactures and produce exhibited, with some remarks on those mineral productions which have served so materially to place our highly-favoured land in the position of the first manufacturing country of the earth.

Coal.—The value of the mineral products of England would be greatly inferior to what it actually is, were it not for the abundant supply of good coal, found in various districts of the kingdom. It will be unnecessary here to point out the many advantages which are derived from the possession of our coal-mines—the source of greater riches than ever issued from the mines of Peru, or from the diamond grounds of India. But for our command of fuel, the inventions of Watt, and Arkwright, would have been of small account; our iron-mines must have long since have ceased to be worked; and nearly every important branch of manufacture which we now possess, must have been rendered impracticable, or, at the least, have been conducted upon a comparatively insignificant scale.

The value of the coal produced annually in Great Britain, is computed at £10,000,000 at the pit's mouth, and at from £15,000,000 to £20,000,000, at the places of consumption. The relative amounts of production of coal of various kinds, in the six principal coal-producing countries of the world, was estimated in 1845, to be as follows:—Great Britain, 31,500,000 tons; Belgium, 4,960,077 tons; United States of America, 4,400,000 tons; France, 4,141,617 tons; Prussia, 3,500,000 tons; Austria, 700,000 tons. Notwithstanding the increasing demand for coal for home consumption, and an augmenting export trade, amounting in 1850 to 3,347,607 tons, or more than three-fourths of the total production of France, the duration of the supply of coal is beyond calculation. The area of the coal-field of South Wales alone, from actual survey, has been estimated at 1,055 square miles, embracing all qualities, from extremely bituminous coal to pure anthracite.

Taking the annual produce of pig iron in the united kingdom at 1,750,000 tons, and supposing that about $3\frac{1}{2}$ tons of coal are required for the production of each ton of iron; the consumption of coal in this branch of the iron trade will, on this hypothesis, amount to 6,123,000 tons per annum; adding to this 3,000,000 tons for the coal required for conversion of pig-iron into bar-iron, it follows, that a supply of not fewer than 9,125,000 tons of coal are annually required in this single department of industry.

The quantity of coals and culm exported, in 1850, was 3,347,607 tons, of the value of £1,280,341; France taking more than any other country; Denmark, Prussia, and the Hanseatic towns coming next in order.

The total quantity of copper raised in the United Kingdom, exceeds 18,000 tons per annum; and the annual supply of tin, from the Cornish mines, is not less than 2,200 tons. From 700 to 1,000 tons of manganese, and 800 to 1,000 tons of arsenic, are annually produced in Cornwall. Of *slate*, 25,000 tons are annually shipped from Cornwall alone, and of *granite*, 22,000 tons. The same county furnishes, to the English and foreign porcelain and earthenware manufactures, 8,000 tons of clay, and 6,000 tons of china stone per annum. Of lead, it is estimated, that the annual production of the country is about 59,000 tons. Many thousand tons of baryta, gypsum, strontia, and other mineral products, are annually raised in this kingdom. The number of bricks, made from the clay of our soil, is upwards of 1,500,000,000 per annum.

Salt.—Among the mineral productions of England, salt has long been an article of considerable importance. Rock salt, is chiefly obtained from the salt mines of Cheshire : whilst our table salt is obtained by the evaporation of the water of the brine springs of Cheshire, Staffordshire, and Worcestershire. In 1801, we made 9,469,491 bushels of salt, of which 1,822,683 were retained for home consumption, and the remainder exported; now, thanks to the repeal of the excise duty in 1825, we make about 28,000,000 bushels of salt per annum, of which about one-half is exported, and the remainder retained for home use; a large portion of which is consumed in the manufacture of soda. We export salt chiefly to the United States of America, our British North American colonies, Russia, Prussia, Belgium, &c.

There is one mineral substance, which we alone possess, and that is, the material of which the Bath brick is made. These are made from the deposit of the River Parrett, in Somersetshire; and as a deposit of similar character is not found anywhere else besides, upwards of 8,000,000 of thos bricks are annually made at Bridgewater, of the value of £12,000 to £13,000, and sent to all parts of the globe. These bricks are as well known in China as in England.

MANUFACTURE OF IRON.
Fabrication de fer—Eisen Manufactur.

AMONG the various manufacturing establishments which our country exhibits, there are few so important, or conducted on so large a scale, as the principal iron works, where the precious metal—iron (more precious, by far, than gold or silver, in relation to the prosperity of a country), is extracted from the crude ore found beneath the soil. In some of the British mines, not only are coal and ironstone dug out of the same pit, but they are actually found together in the same seam or bed. Some of the iron works have the ore beneath them, so as to combine all the operations at one spot; while in others, the ore has to be brought from a distance to the works. The iron ore having been dug from the bowels of the earth, is first roasted, either in a furnace, or in heaps in the open air, by being placed in contact with ignited coal, by which all impurities, which will escape in a gaseous form, are removed. The roasted ore is now placed in the blast furnace, and if it be an argillaceous or clayey ironstone, (which is usually the case), a proportion of limestone is added; to this limestone the term flux is given, its use being, by its superior affinity for clay, to withdraw it from its combination with the metallic iron. If the ore be a calcareous one, clay is used as a flux for the same reasons. To the ore and the flux a quantity of coal or coke is also added, and, as the furnace is previously heated to a high temperature, the iron becomes gradually separated from the clayey material with which it was united, when speedily becoming melted by the intense heat of the furnace, it is then run out, in a liquid state, into moulds of sand; the rough, oblong, pieces of metal thus produced being called "pigs;" the slag or impurities floating on the surface of the melted mass being run into cast-iron boxes, and thence removed to be used for roads, rough walls, and other coarse purposes. The active combustion is kept up in the blast furnace by means of constant blasts of air, forced in through pipes like the nose of a bellows, by a powerful steam engine. In many works, hot air is blown in instead of cold air, and this constitutes the difference between hot and cold blast iron; the air, in the former case, being made to traverse a series of iron pipes, heated from 300° to 600°. The charges or fillings up of ore, flux, and fuel, keep on uninterruptedly three or four times in an hour, for day and night, not suffering further stoppage until the furnace is to be "blown out," either for repairs, or through depression of trade. The furnace is usually tapped, and the liquid mass run out, once in twelve hours.

The "pig-iron" thus obtained, is used for founding and casting, that is, the liquid metal, either direct from the blast furnace, or the pigs subsequently melted in a cupola furnace, is run into moulds of sand, on the floor of the casting-house, these moulds or castings having been constructed in accordance with working drawings: and thus any form or design is obtained in what is termed cast-iron.

The iron thus obtained is not pure iron, it contains a certain portion of carbon, to remove which, in order to form wrought or pure iron, it must be made to undergo various operations. The first of these is termed refining, and consists in placing the pigs of iron, with coal or coke, on the hearth of a furnace, exposing them to the action of an intense heat, and running the liquid metal into moulds of cast-iron, where it is almost instantly chilled, by means of cold water. The refined iron is then put through the puddling or reverberatory furnace, where the remaining carbon and other impurities is driven off, and the former brittle texture of the iron exchanged for one much more malleable and ductile. Lumps of this iron, called "balls or blooms," are then passed under the "shingling hammer," weighing about five tons; next through the "puddle rolls:" a pair of large heavy rollers, working against each other, and having grooves on their surfaces, and are thus formed into bars. These bars are next cut into pieces, piled together in heaps of five or six each, and submitted to a welding heat, in what is termed the *balling furnace*, then taken out and passed through rollers, like the puddling rollers, with grooves of any required form. By this mode of welding five or six bars together, the iron acquires a toughness and malleability it did not previously possess; and in the case of iron, of a superior quality, the same process is conducted a second time. Sheets of iron are made precisely in the same way, the rolls being of such a size, and having such flatness of surface, as will lead to the production of a broad thin sheet, instead of a bar or rod.

The principal seats of the iron manufacture, are Glamorganshire, in South Wales; South Staffordshire, Shropshire, Derbyshire, and the West Riding of Yorkshire, in England; and the district lying eastward of Glasgow, in Scotland.

The following table exhibits the number of iron furnaces in blast, and the number of tons of iron produced by them at different periods:—

In the year	1615,	300 furnaces produced	180,000 tons of iron
"	"	1740,	59	"	"	17,000	"	"
"	"	1806,	121	"	"	250,000	"	"
"	"	1827,	284	"	"	690,000	"	"
"	"	1849,	541	"	"	1,750,000	"	"

The value of the produce of the year 1849, may be estimated at about £15,300,000.

In 1850, there were imported into this country, 45,930 tons of copper ore and regulus; 97,706 cwts. of unwrought and part wrought copper, of which 16,685 cwts. were re-exported; 34,066 tons of unwrought iron, in bars, of which 5,996 tons were re-exported; 49 tons of unwrought steel, and 649 re-exported; 11,977 tons of pig and sheet lead, of which 3,218 tons were re-exported; 18,626 tons of spelter, of which 3,423 tons were re-exported; and 33,332 tons of tin, in blocks, ingots, bars, or slabs, of which 3,795 cwts. were re-exported.

Of metals, the produce of our own country, there were exported in 1850, *Iron*,—142,044 tons of pig, of the value of £347,899; 469,071 tons of bar, bolt, and rod, of the value of £2,795,226; 4,035 tons of wire, of the value of £86,644; 21,201 tons of cast, of the value of £215,396; and 136,514 tons of wrought, of all sorts, of the value of £1,507,971. *Copper,*—154,778 cwts. in bricks and pigs, of the value of £663,579; 253,758 cwts. of sheets, nails, sheathing, &c., to the value of £1,103,858; 13,773 cwts. of wrought, of the value of £71,981; 25,899 cwts. of brass, of all sorts, of the value of £124,350; 22,083 tons of lead, of the value of £387,575; 31,663 cwts. of unwrought tin, of the value of £124,801; and tin plates of the value of £298,928.

Of machinery and mill-work, there were exported in 1850,—steam-engines, and parts of steam-engines, to the value of £424,292. Of all other sorts, to the value of £619,472.

We import copper ore chiefly from Australia, Cuba, and Chili; bar iron, chiefly from Sweden, for the manufacture of steel; lead, from Spain; spelter or zinc, from Prussia, Belgium, and the Hanseatic towns; and tin, from Singapore. We export iron largely to the United States of America, France, Holland, Italy, the Hanseatic towns, Canada, Brazil, &c., &c.; copper, to France, the East Indies, Belgium, and Holland, &c.; lead, to the United States of America, Russia, and the East Indies; tin, to France, Turkey, Russia, Italy, and the United States; and zinc, to the East Indies, and the United States of America.

Berlin is famous for the productions of its iron works; so entirely have the artists of this place, adapted this metal to ornamental purposes, that we are surprised to find it wrought into articles, produced elsewhere only in more costly material; and again into others, hitherto only estimable when manufactured in the most precious metals. All the iron employed at Berlin is English: the English iron being better suited for casting, than any other. Iron properly treated, yields a sharper mould than any other metal, and for the production of all the little graceful *agroupements,* such as we see in Berlin and Paris,—it is not the *technique* or the material that fails us, it is the essential mould, and there is the art.

Near Frankfort is the celebrated iron foundry of Hanau, at which are produced in grey iron, every ornamental article in which iron filagree is in anywise available; and so fine is the workmanship in this hair-wire material, that iron, equivalent in value to one pound sterling, may be manufactured into a variety of articles, amounting in value to one *thousand* pounds. These articles are bracelets, chains, purses, brooches, buckles, clasps, &c., all wrought with a finish so extraordinary, as to excite astonishment, when it is remembered that the material is only iron. Every ornamental object which the French artists and manufacturers produce in bronze, are re-produced in iron, at the works of Hanau, with a measure of success difficult to conceive the material susceptible of.

CHEMICAL PRODUCTS.

Produits Chimiques. Chemische Producte.

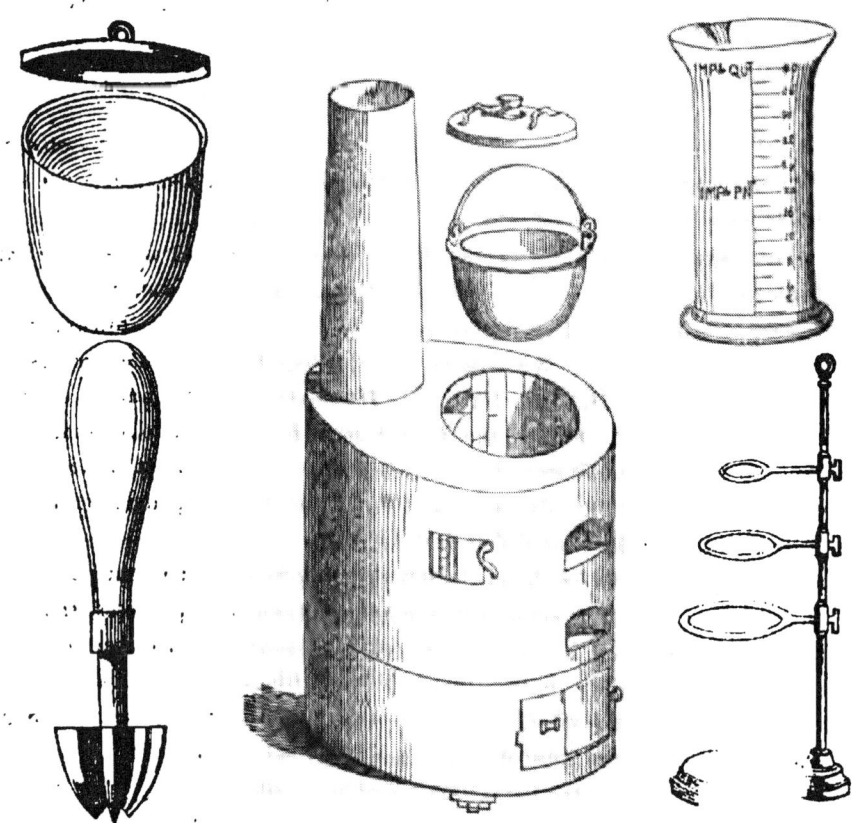

THE chemical discoveries of the last fifty years, have very materially contributed to the immense progress which the arts and manufactures of our country have made during that period of time. An enumeration of a few instances will suffice.

Sulphuric Acid.—The price of this article, which was originally **4s.** per lb., is now to be purchased of the manufacturer, at 1d. per lb. The annual consumption of this acid in Great Britain, is estimated at 70,000 tons, the price of which exercises a great influence on the cost of many of the leading manufactures of our country. In 1838, the quantity of sulphur imported into this country, and chiefly consumed in the manufacture of this acid, was 893,061 cwts. having steadily increased from 251,981 cwts. in

1825, when the absurd attempt made by the Sicilian government to cripple the chief export trade of that country, by the imposition of an export duty of £4 per ton, turned the attention of British chemists to the use of the sulphurets of iron and copper as a source of sulphur in the manufacture of sulphuric acid. In 1839, the importation of sulphur fell to 402,988 cwts., and, though the quantities since imported have varied at different periods, the import of 1838 has never again been attained, though the quantity of sulphuric acid manufactured, has probably more than doubled since that time.

Soda.—This alkali affords another illustration of the great assistance rendered by chemistry to the manufacturer. Formerly, we were dependant for our supply of this alkali on Spain, and Sicily for barilla, and the Highlands of Scotland for kelp; 6,000 tons per annum of the former were imported, and about 25,000 tons of kelp supplied from the northern islands, &c. Now, the principal portion of the soda employed in various manufactures, (such as soap, glass, &c.,) and for domestic and other uses, is obtained from sea salt, and our export alone of this article, amounted, in 1850, to 44,407 tons, of the declared value of £402,129, whilst our import of barilla, diminished to 1,745 tons in the same year. The total quantity annually manufactured in Great Britain, is not short of 200,000 tons, and such is the low price and good quality of this article, as compared with barilla and kelp, that, comparing the relative prices and qualities, a saving of £5,000,000 per annum is effected on the quantity at present made.

Ammonia.—The preparations of ammonia, formerly obtained from animal bones and refuse, are now supplied to us from the coal used in the manufacture of gas, and at so cheap a rate, as to be used for manure.

Amongst some of the chemical preparations, largely imported from abroad, may be mentioned pearlashes or potash, from America and Russia, 184,083 tons; nitrate of potash or saltpetre, from the East Indies, &c., and nitrate of soda, from Chili, to the joint amount of 529,012 tons; whilst Germany and Norway supply us with 1,400 cwts., of cobalt ore or zaffre, and 205,454 lbs. of smalts per annum, the principle consumption of which is for the painting and printing of porcelain and earthenware. Of borax and boracic acid, 19,092 cwts. were imported in 1850.

Phosphorus, which formerly could not be purchased under 30s. per lb., is now manufactured to a considerable extent in this country, and is sold as low as 6s. per lb. The enormous amount of lucifer matches manufactured (estimated at 10,000,000,000), has led to the establishment of works in this country, in which upwards of 20,000 lbs. weight of phosphorus are annually made.

In addition to the various isolated specimens of chemical manufacture exhibited, we would call attention to those exhibited by Mr. Button, which, for purity and excellence of manufacture, stand unrivalled.

This collection consists of a series of acids, such as boracic, chromic, metagallic, phosphoric, and uric acids; also, four of the principal alums, viz., ammonia, chrome, potash, and soda alum. Several salts of ammonia, in particular the oxalate and binoxalate of ammonia, placed under glass shades, are remarkable for size of crystals.

Also a series of salts of the different metals and metallic earths, such as the salts of arsenic, barium, bismuth, cadmium, calcium, cerium, cobalt, copper, glucina, iron, lead, manganese, mercury, nickel, potash, soda, silver, strontia, tin, tungsten, uranium, and zinc.

To the chemical philosopher, intent on his researches on the hidden properties and qualities of bodies—to the physician, anxious to alleviate the ills of suffering humanity—to the manufacturer, dyer, calico printer, and bleacher, each alive to the necessity of progress,—continued progress, in the sphere of their respective operations, the quality of the various tests and re-agents employed by them is of paramount importance.

The engravings are selected from Mr. Button's interesting and compendious catalogue of chemical apparatus, lately published, to which we refer our readers for full information on the subject of chemical apparatus.

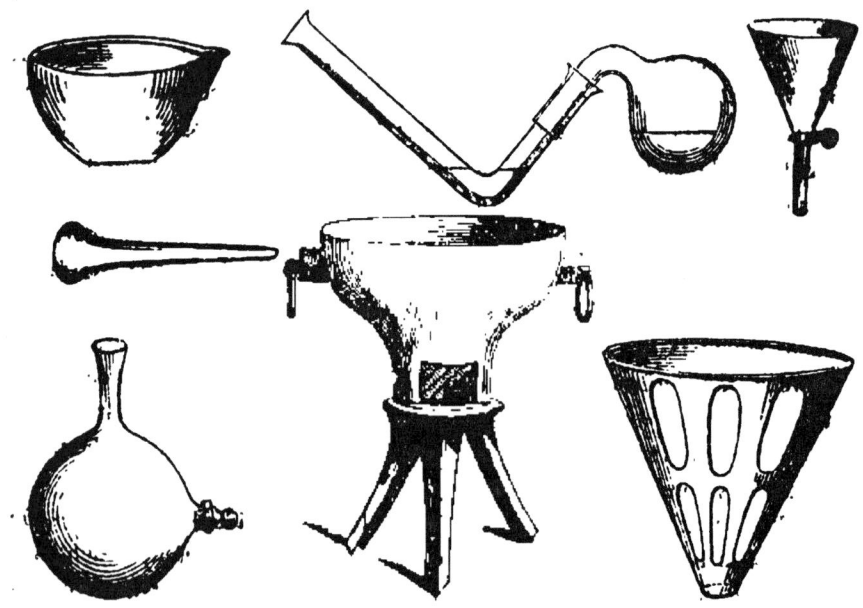

MANUFACTURE OF SOAP.

Fabrication du Savon.   Bereitung von Seife.

THE manufacture of soap is an entirely chemical process. The barilla, as imported into this country, or the soda ash, manufactured in Great Britain, is first rendered caustic, by solution in water, with quick or caustic lime; the lime takes by its superior affinity, the carbonic acid present in the barilla or soda ash (which is a carbonate of soda), and precipitates in the form of carbonate of lime or chalk, while the caustic soda remains in solution. This solution is then boiled, either with olive oil, tallow, palm, or cocoa-nut oils, and with or without resin, and other ingredients, and the resulting mixture poured into large vessels or frames, made of wood or iron, formed of rectangular plates or bars, which, when the soap has cooled, and become hard, are taken apart, and the mass or block of soap thus obtained is cut into bars, or moulded into cakes, as may be required. Perfumes or colours are added to the soap, just before or after the liquid soap is placed in the frames. This is what is usually called hard soap. Soft soap is made by using a caustic solution of potash or pearlashes, instead of soda, with seed or fish oil and tallow.

In the manufacture of fancy or scented soaps, it is usual to stamp the name of the maker on the soap, indenting the same by means of a suitable stamp; this, however, being very superficial, becomes entirely defaced after the soap has been used a few times. Mr. Dunn, soap manufacturer, of Worcester, considering it important, both to the manufacturer and the consumer, that the latter should know by whom the soap was manufactured, has devised a method of marking such soap with the maker's name, in such a way that it cannot be obliterated like the ordinary stamp mark. For this purpose, he stamps the cakes of soap in the usual manner, but uses a stamp penetrating to a considerable depth in the soap; the mark thus formed he fills up with soap of a different colour to that of the stamped cake, which is introduced either in a plastic state, or in the state of fine powder, the surface being covered with moist soap, of the same colour as the powder introduced. The coloured soap so inlaid, will wear away with the surface of the soap, and yet present the maker's name, until the piece be entirely consumed.

The quantity of soap made in Great Britain, in 1850, was 157,254,000 lbs., exclusive of the quantity made and consumed in Ireland, which pays no excise duty. Quantity of soap exported, was 124,038 cwts., of the declared value of £201,374. The quantity of soap imported into Great Britain from Ireland, in 1849, was 200,178 lbs.

MANUFACTURE OF CANDLES.

Fabrication des Bougies. Bereitung von Lichten.

WE are indebted to the researches of M. Chevreul, of Paris, for the great improvements which have been introduced into the manufacture of candles. This distinguished chemist found that, by proper treatment, the soft part or oleine of tallow might be separated from the hard part, the stearine or stearic acid, by which means a substance, resembling wax in hardness, and the good quality of not being greasy to the touch, might be obtained, well adapted for the manufacture of candles. The more modern existing improvements in the candle manufacture, may be said to have arisen out of the introduction of improved processes for obtaining the stearic acid of tallow, and the combination with it of the stearine of cocoa-nut oil, now largely imported into this country for this purpose. It was found, that when the vegetable stearine of the cocoa-nut was combined with the stearic acid of the tallow, in about equal proportions, a candle might be produced, which might be burned with a plaited wick, so as to require no snuffing. This combination was the invention of Mr. James Wilson, one of the managing partners in Messrs. Price and Company's Candle Works, at Vauxhall, and the candle was appropriately named " composite."

The faculty of throwing off the exhausted portion of the wick (that is, the snuff), belongs exclusively to the plaited wick. Owing to the twist, this portion of the wick turns out of the flame of the candle into the atmospheric draught, which ascends on all sides around it, and is thus carried off. Such a wick, however, can only be used in conjunction with a firm substance, like the mixture above mentioned, and this advantage has secured for the composite candles an immense demand.

As a general rule, the more solid the tallow, the more valuable is it for the manufacture of candles, and this quality of the fat has been found by experience to be greatest in animals fed upon dry ripe fodder. Hence, the tallow which comes from Russia, where the animals are fed for eight months in the year on dry fodder, is generally superior to that produced at home.

The quantity of tallow imported in 1850, was 1,241,781 cwts., of which 1,216,101 were entered for home consumption. Quantity of palm oil imported 448,589 cwts., and of cocoa-nut oil 98,040 cwts. Quantity of candles exported 2,723,531 lbs., of the declared value of £98,108.

SIR W. BURNETT & CO.'S PATENT PROCESS FOR THE PRESERVATION OF WOOD, CANVAS, &c. FROM DRY-ROT.

Procédé Breveté pour la Conservation des Bois, du Canevas, &c.
Bewahrung des Holzes und Leinwand gegen Verfaulung.

In addition to the home-grown timber, felled in our own country, during 1850, no less than 1,700,000 loads of foreign timber, imported principally from the Baltic, and British North America, were entered for home consumption, in addition to 80,000 loads of foreign and colonial staves; and when it is considered that the value of this timber is not short of £5,000,000, it at once becomes evident, that any process which can impart a preservative power to timber, and prevent its speedy decay, must be of great value. Experience has shown, that when wood is exposed to the simultaneous influence of air and moisture, it gradually undergoes decomposition and decay. The decomposition of the fibres of the wood may take place in at least two conditions, viz., in the moist state subject to the free access of air, and under the surface of water, when the air obtains access only by being dissolved in the water. If the wood is perfectly exposed to the air, it may suffer another kind of decomposition, known as the dry rot, by which it is rendered brittle, and has its cohesion completely destroyed.

In damp and ill-ventilated situations, the dry rot produces the most serious results, causing, in a few years, the destruction of entire buildings and ships. But though favoured by a damp and close atmosphere, it may occur where the ventilation is perfect, and the atmosphere in its usual state of humidity.

The albuminous matter which wood contains distributed over the cellular tissue, is intimately connected with the decomposition and decay of the wood. It is in the highest degree putrescible, and, therefore, an element of fermentation and putrefaction. It is also particularly adapted as food for insects, which are often found in the interior of the cells, penetrating the wood in all directions in search of it. This disintegration of the fibres, greatly facilitates the chemical action which speedily supervenes, from the increased facility afforded for the introduction of air and moisture; ammonia and ammoniacal salts are developed, and these favour the growth of fungi, which are consequently among the earliest signs of the decay of wood.

These fungi insert their filaments into every crevice of the wood, and being of excessive fineness, readily pass down and between the tubes from which the wood is organized, forcing them asunder, and thus gradually, but completely destroying the cohesion of the tissue; and as the development and growth of these filaments increase with great rapidity and force, the total ruin of the timber speedily ensues.

To prevent this decomposition of the fibre, and the consequent destruction of the wood, the latter is usually dried by exposure to a free current of air for a considerable period, or is rendered perfectly dry by the aid of heat; this, however, does not remove the vegetable albumen. A considerable time is required for drying by exposure to the air; and wood, rendered perfectly dry by the aid of heat, when exposed at common temperatures to the atmosphere, in its ordinary state of humidity, reabsorbs a certain proportion of water, varying according to the compactness of the wood. As long as well-seasoned wood can be kept perfectly dry, it is not subject to dry-rot; it is, however, capable of absorbing sufficient moisture from the air to continue the decomposition when once commenced by contact with diseased timber, or otherwise. The albumen may, indeed, be removed from the wood by washing, but in addition to the length of time required for that process, the adhesion of the fibre, and consequent tenacity of the wood, is thereby much diminished.

The most effectual method of preserving timber, is to cause the albumen to enter into combination with some other substance, capable of forming with it a compound, insoluble in water, and not liable to spontaneous decomposition.

For this purpose, Sir H. Davy recommended to the Admiralty and Navy Board, the employment of corrosive sublimate; but the solution of this salt being found to be slightly volatile at common temperatures, it was considered that the atmosphere surrounding the prepared timbers might become vitiated, and the proposal was therefore not carried into effect. Subsequently, Mr. Kyan, patented the application of corrosive sublimate, for the preservation of wood, but the expense of the preparation, and other circumstances, have led to the abandonment of the process. A variety of other preservative agents have been tried, but on the ground of expense and other reasons, there is none which holds the place in public estimation which chloride of zinc has obtained. The use of this salt as a preservative of wood, was patented by Sir William Burnett, in 1838; it acts like corrosive sublimate, by forming an insoluble compound with the vegetable albumen, with the additional advantage of perfect innocuity, and of forming a compound with albumen, which, unlike that formed by corrosive sublimate, is insoluble in sea water. The severe testing to which the chloride of zinc has been submitted during the last twelve years, proves, that in the present state of our chemical knowledge, as a preservative agent, it is unequalled.

As a preservative agent for railway sleepers, the chloride of zinc has not been surpassed. Mr. S. M. Peto, the eminent railway contractor, states, that some Scotch fir sleepers, prepared for him by Sir W. Burnett's process, and which were laid down on one of the lines of railway executed by him in 1841, were, in 1849, in as perfectly sound a state as when they were first laid, whilst those that were put down in juxta-position with them at the same time, unprepared, are quite decayed. So perfectly satisfied is Mr. Brunel, the eminent engineer of the Great Western Railway, with the preservative efficacy of the chloride of zinc, that he has adopted its application to all the works under his management.

Mr. Adams, of Gosport, architect, reports as regards the use of the chloride of zinc, as a preservative of wooden flooring, that in the erection of two churches, and two school houses, built respectively, eight, seven, six, and five years since, he caused the boards of the ground flooring to be saturated with the chloride of zinc, and that it has proved perfectly successful. In one of the instances, indeed, the ground from its moist nature, was of a description to hasten more than usually the decay of flooring laid next above it; yet the boards of this, as well as the other three buildings, continue in a sound and perfect state.

Another great advantage arising from the employment of chloride of zinc, is that of allowing the use of some of the cheaper kinds of timber, as beech, elm, Scotch fir, &c., as substitutes for oak. Mr. Hacker, the superintendent of works on the estate of the Duke of Bedford, at Woburn, gives as the result of his experiments, that whilst the Burnettized pieces of beech, Scotch fir, larch, and elm, all remained perfectly sound, the unprepared elm, beech, and Scotch fir, were thoroughly rotten.

At the Royal Hospital, Haslar, prepared timber, which, in 1836, was put to replace some that had been removed in a complete state of dry rot, with immense fungi attached, was found in 1848, to be in a perfectly clean and sound state, there being no particle of fungus to be seen.

The Burnettized wood has also been proved, at Calcutta, to resist the destructive ravages of the white ant, in a situation where unprepared timber was completely riddled by them.

It was at first feared, that the iron nails driven into wood, prepared with chloride of zinc, might become more speedily oxidized than when inserted in unprepared wood; the researches, however, of Mr. Mitchell, engineer at the Royal Dockyard, Sheerness, go to prove, that the "preparation does not hasten the oxidation of metal, and in comparison with unprepared wood, appears to retard it."

The result of some trials made with this solution, by the Earl of Charleville, is as follows: "All the timber so prepared has a very satisfactory appearance; I consider it quite as good for *seasoning* timber, and *preferable to the solution of corrosive sublimate for timber that is to be worked on the bench*. It does not leave that gritty substance on the surface that is left from corrosive sublimate, which is so injurious to the plane irons. I have also had a large quantity of small poles or tops prepared, principally of Scotch fir, from one-and-a-half to three inches in diameter, consequently, they are nearly all sap. They have been in use about two years, in what is commonly called American paling. I find, on examining them, that they are as sound between wind and water, as when put into the ground."

The chloride of zinc has also been most successfully applied to the preservation of the electric telegraph posts, and also to hop poles, which, when prepared, are found to be thrice as durable as those which have not been submitted to the preservative process.

The chloride of zinc also communicates, to some extent, the quality of incombustibility to wood prepared with it; on this subject the Secretary of the Admiralty made the following communication to Sir W. Burnett: " My Lords Commissioners of the Admiralty having caused experiments to be made, to test the incombustibility of woods, when saturated in your solution, I am commanded by their lordships to acquaint you, that it has been ascertained, that the soft woods, such as yellow pine and other deals, both foreign and English, saturated with the solution prepared in certain proportions, when exposed to the immediate contact of iron, heated to a blood-red heat, did not at all ignite into flame, whereas, unprepared wood of the same kind, burst into flame immediately."

In consequence of this report, the Admiralty have ordered the bulkheads in the holds, and magazines in her Majesty's ships, to be fitted with timber so saturated, and it is also applied largely to the various buildings in her Majesty's dockyards.

It has also been satisfactorily proved, by a series of carefully conducted experiments, that the chloride of zinc produces with the albumen of the wood, a compound, insoluble even in boiling water, and Professors Brande, Graham, and Cooper, have all reported most favourably on the use of the chloride of zinc, not only as a preservative of wood, but also of cordage, canvas, hides, and other vegetable and animal substances. Of the value of the chloride of zinc as a preservative agent for canvas, woollen, &c. no addition need be offered to the following testimony of the eminent shipbuilder the late Mr. Somes, and that of the practical researches of Mr. Toplis.

Mr. Somes said, " I have had upwards of 23,000 yards of 'Burnettized' canvas in use, as awnings and sails, on board of my ships, in all quarters of the globe—the greater part of which have been in wear, more than three years, in India and China; and I find, on their return to this country, that they are invariably free from mildew, and, comparatively in a good state of preservation. Having experienced such beneficial results from the adoption of Sir W. Burnett's process, I shall use it more extensively, and recommend it with the greatest confidence."

Mr. Toplis states as follows: "I have, for my own satisfaction, made some few experiments, with a view to determine the *preservative power of* the chloride, under circumstances likely to give considerable confidence in the permanency of the salutary change operated upon the organic structure. I took two separate pieces of the same woollen cloth, one of which had been immersed for forty-eight hours in the solution of chloride of zinc, then dried, and afterwards washed in cold water; the other piece in its ordinary unprepared state; both were then subjected to a similar process of dyeing, in the course of which operation they both *remained in the boiling fluid*, for some time (say twenty minutes). The two pieces were subsequently buried in the earth of a melon frame, and taken thence at the end of fourteen days. The unprepared piece was in a state of complete decay; the prepared piece retained its original strength of texture and colour. These specimens were placed in your hands. I have now the pleasure of sending you two pieces of sail-cloth which have been treated in the same way, and with similar results. The time they remained in the earth was three weeks.

These experiments will, I conceive, go very far to remove any doubts which might be raised as to the *permanency* of the preservative power of chloride of zinc on animal and vegetable fibre; since the boiling in the dye-vat, subsequently to preparation, may well be supposed to have removed from the cloth whatever was left soluble in water, by the previous maceration in the dissolved chloride.

In my own mind, not the smallest doubt exists, that a permanent chemical union takes place, as I have before intimated, between the organic fibre and the metallic base of the salt; and that to such union must be ascribed the new power, now so frequently and so satisfactorily ascertained, of resisting decomposition under circumstances well known to induce the premature decay of animal and vegetable fibrous structures."

The chloride of zinc also acts as a powerful preservative of woollen cloths and furs against the ravages of moths. Mr. Morton, of the Admiralty, found that not only were prepared cloths and furs untouched by the moths, but that the moths which were in the chest previous to the introduction of the prepared cloths and furs, were speedily destroyed.

APPARATUS EMPLOYED IN SIR W. BURNETT & Co.'s PATENT
PROCESS FOR THE PRESERVATION OF WOOD, CANVAS, &c.

*Appareil à l'usage du procédé Breveté, pour la Conservation des Bois,
du Canevas, &c.*

*Apparat welches in dem Process gebraucht wird für die Bewahrung des
Holzes und Leinwand gegen Verfaulung.*

———

SIMPLE immersion, or steeping of the wood in the solution of chloride of
zinc, though applicable in some cases, is by no means so efficient a mode of
preparing the timbers, as that by atmospheric pressure. Whenever it is required to "Burnettize" timber, railway sleepers, masts for ships, &c., in
large quantities, economically and efficiently, the improved apparatus manufactured for this purpose, by Messrs. James Burton and Sons, engineers of
Holland-street, Southwark, should be employed. This apparatus consists
of a wrought-iron cylinder, of any required size, with mouth-piece and
cover the whole diameter of the cylinder, perfectly air-tight, and capable
of sustaining a vacuum, of not less than 29° or 28° at least; and also a
pressure of 150 to 200 pounds on the square inch. The cylinder is fitted
with a tram-way, made to run the whole length, for the conveyance of the
loaded trucks or carriages entering the cylinder with the wood to be operated upon. There is also a traversing railway, with a double line of rails,
running the whole length of the cylinder, so constructed, that it receives
the prepared wood on one line of rails, and being then moved transversely,
it allows of another charge of timber to be prepared, being introduced into
the cylinder; a considerable saving is thus effected, both in time and labour.
The apparatus is worked by a steam engine, provided with double-acting
vacuum and pressure pumps, (*see engraving*). The cylinder being
charged with the timber to be prepared, the cover is fitted on, and the air
contained in the cylinder, and in the pores of the wood, is withdrawn by the
vacuum pump, and the solution of chloride of zinc, injected into the cylinder, by means of the powerful pressure pump. In this way the operation
is most efficiently performed, the solution thus penetrating large pieces of
timber, and completely saturating them with the preservative fluid.

Some of Messrs. Burton's cylinders, fitted with pumps, &c. complete, are
fixed and in use in Her Majesty's Dockyards; these cylinders are 6 feet in

Fig. 5.

diameter, and 85 feet in length, and are employed for Burnettizing the masts of ships, &c. Messrs. Burton and Sons, have also made cylinders for the East India Company, the Russian Government, &c., which have been highly approved.

When smaller cylinders are required for moveable stations, small engines mounted on wheels are used, and are found extremely economical, as well as convenient for the above and other similar purposes. The engraving below represents one of these engines, as manufactured by Messrs. Burton and Sons.

Railway contractors and others having sleepers and timber to prepare on different parts of a line of railway, will find this portable injecting apparatus very convenient, often saving them a considerable amount of labour and expense which would be incurred in taking the timber to a fixed station, and again moving it to the point where its use was required.

GALVANIZED IRON.

Fer Galvanisé.   Verzinktes Eisen.

It is well known, that iron, when placed in contact with water, or exposed to a damp atmosphere, becomes oxidated ; the oxide of iron thus produced, having a pulverulent form, becomes readily removed by the action of the rain, and new surfaces of the metal thus becoming continually exposed to the oxidating effects of the atmosphere, the whole of the iron gradually rusts and is destroyed.

The preservation of iron from rust, occupied the attention, and exercised the ingenuity of scientific and practical men for a long series of years. A variety of processes were suggested and adopted, but none were found to stand the test of time, or prove applicable to the great variety of purposes for which it was required.

When zinc is exposed to the action of water or a damp atmosphere, a process of oxidation likewise takes place ; but the oxide of zinc formed, being of close and uniform texture, adheres to the surface of the metal, forming a protective coating against the further oxidating influences of the atmosphere. The softness of zinc, and its liability to expansion and contraction when exposed to changes of the temperature, renders its useful employment very limited. Such being the case, the idea suggested itself to the mind of M. Sorel, of applying the principle of galvanic protection to the iron, by coating it with metallic zinc, thus combining the strength and durability of the iron, with the quality of resistance to increasing oxidation possessed by the zinc. The practical result of this combination proved eminently successful, and an experience of seven years in this country, and of double that period in France, has established beyond a doubt the fact, that iron subjected to this patent process of galvanizing or coating with pure zinc, is capable of offering effectual resistance to the action of the atmosphere, and of water, whether fresh or salt, under all conceivable conditions.

The application of the process, independently of its being of the highest importance, is, in truth, conducive to real economy, as, from the permanent protection it affords, the necessity of paint, or other modes of preservation (none of which are really effectual), is entirely superseded.

In consequence of the great success attending the use of the galvanized iron, prepared according to Craufurd's patent, of which Messrs. Tupper and

Carr, of Mansion House-street, are the proprietors; the demand for its use has, of late years, become very extensive, both in this country and abroad, and the varied improvements from time to time introduced by the proprietors into the patent process, have rendered its application increasingly extensive.

It has been used for the entire roofing (many acres) of the New Palace at Westminster; the building slips in Her Majesty's Dockyards at Deptford, Woolwich, Chatham, Sheerness, Pembroke, Portsmouth, and Devonport; and has been adopted by many of the railway companies for covering sheds, and stations,—particularly the Lime-street, and Waterloo-street stations, Liverpool; the workshops at Swindon, on the Great Western Railway, &c. In the colonies, and in tropical climates, it has been found peculiarly valuable, superseding all other kinds of roofing, from its not being liable to contraction or expansion, like zinc or lead.

A most important application of the Patent Galvanized Iron, is that of sheathing for vessels,—experienced persons considering it much more suitable than either yellow metal or copper for sheathing *iron-fastened vessels*, and also much cheaper; the loss in weight, and depreciation in price, of yellow metal or copper, at the end of three years, together with interest and insurance on additional outlay, amounting to more than the original cost of the galvanized iron. Galvanized iron nails and bolts, for fastenings, when not in contact with copper, have been proved to possess great durability; nails and bolts of this description, also, do not injure the timbers or planking, by producing what is usually termed "*iron sickness.*"

The barque *Oregon*, 338 tons register, the property of Mr. Mc Lachlan, of Liverpool, was sheathed with the patent galvanized iron early in 1846, since which she has made two voyages, one to Patagonia, calling round by Rio de Janeiro and Bahia, and back to Liverpool; and another, from Liverpool to Quebec and back, the two voyages occupying about twenty months. On inspecting her, the sheathing was found to be in such good condition, that she was sent on a voyage to Callao and back with the same metal on, and so satisfied was the owner with the wear of the galvanized iron, that he has had the brig *Sirius*, 286 tons register, sheathed with it, considering it the best and cheapest metal for vessels partly iron and copper-fastened, and for second and third-class vessels.

The *Enterprise* and the *Investigator* were sheathed with galvanized iron, which, on their return home, was found to be in such good condition, that the vessels were despatched on their second voyage with the metal on.

The Lords Commissioners of the Admiralty have also ordered the coal bunkers of the Government steamers to be fitted up with galvanized iron.

The galvanized iron sheathing appears also to repel the attachment of barnacles and vegetable matter to the ship's hull, which prove so serious an obstacle to the vessel's progress through the water. The leading advantages possessed by the patent galvanized iron sheathing over copper and yellow metal are, first, a saving of at least one-third in the cost of material; secondly, increased strength is secured by the use of iron instead of copper bolts; thirdly, its applicability to copper as well as iron-fastened vessels, for if the copper bolts are isolated by a covering of felt or strong brown paper, soaked in a preparation of shellac dissolved in essential oil of tar, the galvanic action of the metals is entirely prevented.

Amongst the more recent applications of the patent galvanized iron in the construction of various public works, within the last few months, may be mentioned the whole of the louvre or ventilating plates (in number about 13,000) of the Great Exhibition Building in Hyde Park, and for roofing the Great Central Gas Company's premises at Bow Common.

The Electric Telegraph Company have adopted the patent galvanized iron for the telegraph wires through all their extended operations, with uniform success; and the following railway companies have employed it in the telegraphs erected by them during the last six months, viz.: London and Brighton; Reading, Guilford and Reigate; Ashford and Hastings; Bow and Blackwall; Oxford and Banbury; Chester and Holyhead; and Chester and Birkenhead.

Amongst other useful applications of the galvanized iron, may be mentioned that of the moulds, &c., employed in the manufacture of refined sugar. It came out, in the investigation of Dr. Scoffern's process for refining sugar by means of salts of lead, that in the process at present employed, moulds painted with white lead are used, and that there is danger of the sugar being contaminated with lead from this cause. All such danger is obviated by the use of galvanized iron.

Furnace pans, made of galvanized iron, are admirably adapted for the humbler classes, inasmuch as they are cheap, cleanly, and not so liable to be stolen as copper.

A long list may be given of the different purposes to which the galvanized iron has been successfully applied; amongst them may be mentioned wire fencing, wire ropes, anchors, and the general fittings of a ship, chains, coal-scuttles, coopers' hoops, chimney pots, dahlia rods, fly wires, flower frames and stands, guttering, girders, gas and water pipes, gratings, garden chairs, green-houses, iron hurdles, nails, &c., &c. In short, there is scarcely any use to which iron can be put, which does not admit of the application of this useful process.

APPARATUS FOR DISTILLATION, &c.

Appareil Distillatoire.   *Apparat zum Distilliren.*

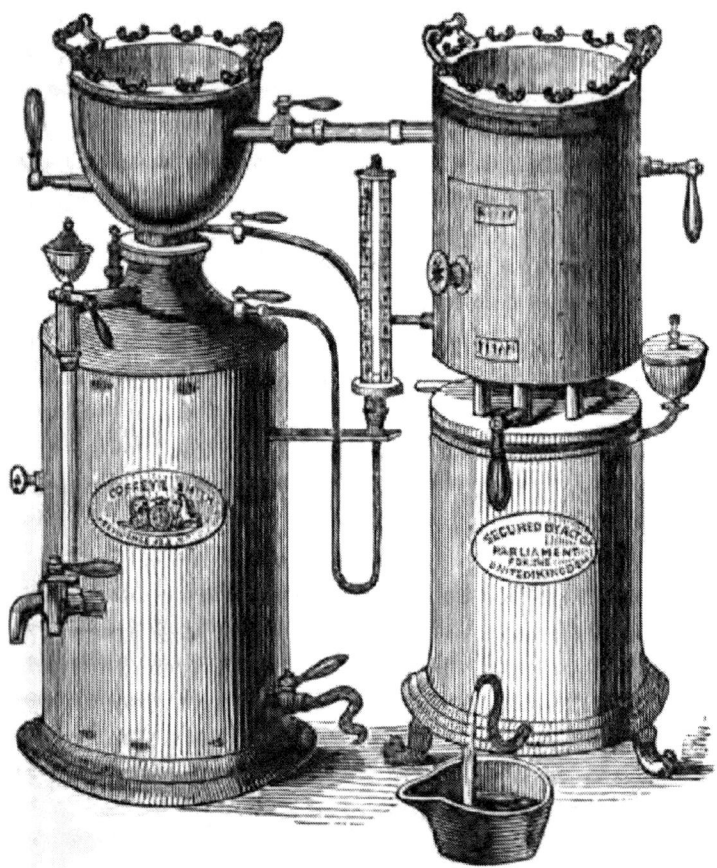

WE doubt whether the visitors to the exhibition will find, throughout the whole range of scientific apparatus submitted to their inspection, so ingenious and complete a still as the Esculapian still of Messrs. Coffey and Smith, above illustrated. If labour, time, command of operations, economy, and simplicity, are any recommendations, a still, which, in its construction and working, combines these advantages, and that, too, in an eminent degree, is worthy of especial recommendation. Here, in the space of a few square feet, is presented to us an apparatus, which, while performing the office of an ordinary stove, contains a still, condenser, two, three, or four evaporating and decocting pans, steam bath, (for retort), drying closet, &c., ready for use at any time or season. The great reduction in the price of gas enables it to be used as a clean and economical source of heat, and the heat thus obtained can be regulated with the greatest nicety, and raised to 300° Fah. if required. The economy of fuel is very great, as the steam required to work the pans, closets, retorts, &c., is condensed, yielding a copious supply of pure distilled water. The still is also easy of management, and devoid of danger. The condenser is a great improvement upon the old plan, inasmuch as it is two-thirds more powerful in refrigerating power, and can be readily taken asunder, washed, and put together again in a few minutes. The whole contrivance is admirably adapted for the operations of the chemist and pharmaceutist, as well as for all general purposes requiring the use of such an apparatus.

APPARATUS FOR THE PRODUCTION OF ARTIFICIAL ICE, AND THE PREPARATION OF ICE CREAMS, &c.

Appareil pour la fabrication de la Glace artificielle et la preparation des Glaces.

Apparät zur Kunstlichen, Bereitung von Eis, &c.

WHILST objects of every class, calculated to supply the wants and increase the comforts of the human race, arrest the attention of the visitor, the exhibition is not entirely deficient in those objects which minister to the gratification of the inner man. Whilst exercising the greatest possible ingenuity in the construction of that wondrous mechanism, which has placed our country in such a proud position amongst the manufacturing nations of the earth, the application of this ingenuity to the every-day wants and comforts of domestic life, has, until a very recent period, been almost entirely overlooked. A step, however, has now been taken in that direction, the *avant-courier* of new and more important improvements; and to no one are we more indebted than to Mr. Masters, for various useful and interesting contrivances in domestic economy. Mr. Masters exhibits quite a museum of apparatus, as varied in their uses as in form, all displaying considerable ingenuity and skill, and a happy adaptation of means to the end in view.

The Ice Machine is constructed for the purpose of forming artificial ice in a few minutes, for preparing dessert ices, cooling wines, &c. The researches of Mr. Walker, of Cambridge, and other scientific men, have enabled us to form such mixtures of saline substances as, by their liquefaction, produce an intensity of cold previously unknown; if, for instance, we dissolve 5 parts of muriate of ammonia (sal ammoniac), and 5 parts of nitrate of potash (saltpetre), in 16 parts of water, so great a degree of cold is thereby produced, that the mercury in the thermometer falls from 50° above zero, to from 10° to 40° below zero, or from 42° to 72° below the freezing point of water. Mr. Masters prepares a saline compound, capable of producing, when dissolved in water, a greater degree of cold than that obtained from the employment of any previously known mixture, reducing water from a temperature of 132° to 32°,—the freezing point.

Plate 1, shows the freezing and cooling machine, as ready for action. It consists of an outer case, forming a cellaret or wine cooler below, whilst the upper division contains the necessary apparatus for the operation of freezing; consisting of a freezer, made of pure white metal, into which

Plate 1.   Plate 3.

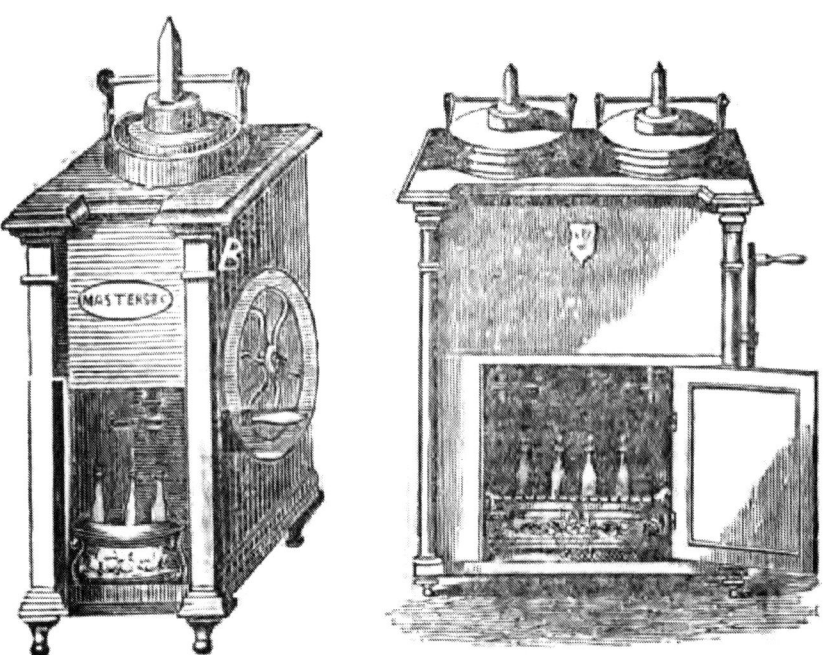

is introduced the dessert ice to be congealed, with a space surrounding the outside of the freezer, completely filled with the freezing mixture, the exterior boundary of such space being formed by the introduction of a metallic cylinder, nearly filled with *pure spring water;* the whole is surrounded by the exterior case, and protected as much as possible from the influence of conduction and radiation, by means of non-conducting materials, properly selected and disposed. The freezer, containing the cream, &c., is made to revolve, by means of the handle attached to the side of the machine; the freezing mixture acts quickly upon it and its

contents, while a fixed spatula, in the interior of the machine, removes
the congealed cream from the sides of the freezer, keeping the whole
substance in a complete state of agitation, and thus preventing the ingredients separating one from the other. The effect thus produced, in an
incredibly short space of time, (three or four minutes only being required),
on the quality and character of the ices is truly astonishing, and such as
could hardly be expected. The fine and homogeneous character of the
article produced, surpasses all that can be accomplished by hand, whilst
the extreme simplicity of the machine, and the economy of the process,
are by no means its least recommendation. The machine may be charged
also without the dessert ice, or without the spring water, when the water
in the metallic case is alone required to be frozen. In this case, a block
of solid ice may be obtained, which, by suitable contrivances, may be
beautifully decorated with fruits or flowers, and thus made to present a
very pleasing appearance.

Plate 3, represents a double freezing machine, in which two kinds of
dessert ice may be prepared at the same time.

Plate 4, represents the "patent preserving safe, or cooling apparatus."
It consists of a double lined box, fitted with metallic lining, so constructed,
as to allow the cooling power to percolate through the interior, the inner

Plate 4.   *Plate* 4.

The Patent Ice Safe when closed.   The Patent Ice Safe with doors open.

The Patent Ice Safe contains an Ice Well in the centre, with a Water Well by which water
may be constantly kept cold. The closets at each end and the drawers at the bottom
are for preserving Game, Fish, &c. from the effects of heat, and for cooling wine, &c.
An Air Pump is fixed to the side for exhausting hot air when required.

case being carefully provided against loss, by means of suitable non-conducting substances. The upper portion of this machine is a reservoir,
for containing the cooling power, ice, &c. This is introduced, and allowed
to remain for any length of time required. As the ice or mixture passes
into solution, it is conducted, by pipes, throughout the whole interior

surface, trays, &c., eventually escaping by the tap, represented at the lower portion of the machine. Curiously enough, this contrivance may also serve the purpose of a warming apparatus; for which purpose, it is only necessary to supply hot water, in the place of the cooling mixture.

Plate 5.

Masters' Patent Sherry Cobbler Freezing and Cooling Jug, for producing pure Ice from Spring Water, on the table or sideboard, in 5 minutes, at the cost of 2d., in the hottest climate.

Plate 6.

Masters' Patent Butter Cooler and Freezer.

Plate 8.

Masters' Patent Cooling Decanter or Claret Jug.

Plate 7.

Masters' Patent Iceing Percolating Funnel for regulating the temperature of water, wine, &c. in a few minutes, without ice, at the cost of one halfpenny.

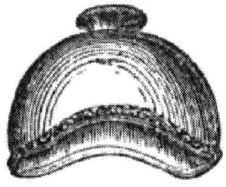

Patent Cooling Cap for surgical purposes.

Mr. Masters, has made a very useful application of his freezing process, to the formation of an ice helmet, which will prove a very valuable aid to the medical man, in cases when the application of cold to the head is requisite to afford relief in certain diseases. Like the before mentioned vessels, it is double. The freezing mixture is introduced in the cavity between, and after a few seconds' agitating, it may be applied. The inconvenience attendant on the application of ice to the head is very great; hence, from the simplicity of the above contrivance, the helmet will be duly appreciated.

APPARATUS FOR THE AERATION OF LIQUIDS AND THE MANUFACTURE OF SODA WATER, LEMONADE, &c.

Appareil pour l'aérification des liquides, et la préparation de l'Eau de Seltz, Limonade Gazeuse, &c.

Apparat für die aëration von Flüssigheiten und zur Bereitung von Soda Wasser.

MANY and various have been the forms of apparatus devised for aërating waters, or impregnating them with carbonic acid, with a view to furnish a cool, sparkling, refreshing beverage in summer.

None of these apparatus however, have obtained more than a short-lived celebrity, some defect either in principle or construction have rendered them useless. Mr. Masters has invented an aërated water machine, which, from its portability, correctness of principle, and peculiarity of construction, is destined to obtain considerable popularity. By its aid we may in a few minutes, prepare any aërated water we please, nor are we confined to waters only,—all other beverages, no matter of what description, are as easily prepared. To this apparatus is attached no unwieldly appurtenances,—the whole machine, generator, and receiver, occupying but the space of a small table vase, or decanter.

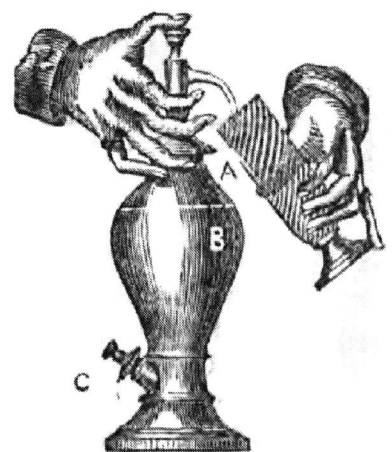

The apparatus, in its various modifications is extremely simple, and so contrived as to require but a very small amount of attention or manipulation. With it, a child may as easily prepare soda water, as any other person, and quite as effectually, for it is impossible to err in the preparation, the machine being almost an automaton.

Mr. Masters has contrived a variety of different forms of aërating apparatus, all of them however, depending on the same principle, viz., the liberation of carbonic acid gas from bicarbonate of soda, by means of tartaric acid; the absorption of this carbonic acid by the water, soda water, beer, or any other fluid which it may be required to render brisk and effervescing, and the withdrawal of the same from the apparatus for use whenever required.

The annexed plate shows the apparatus in its simplest form. C is the gas generator, and B the part of the apparatus containing the liquid to be aërated, whence it is drawn off for use as required.

The aërated water machines, are composed of glass, earthenware, and porcelain, and are very economical, enabling us to obtain a pure article of soda water, lemonade, or other similar beverage, at a very trifling cost, after the first outlay for the apparatus.

The following are some of the varied forms which the ingenuity and taste of Mr. Masters has given to the aërated water apparatus.

KNIFE CLEANING MACHINES.

Machine pour Nettoyer les Couteaux.   Maschine zam Messer putzen.

By means of these useful machines, constructed according to Mr. Masters'
recent improvements, knives may be cleaned and polished, in an incredibly
short space of time.   During the process, the operator has not to
undergo the inconvenience of dust and noise, usually attendant on the
old process, and the ivory handles are no longer discoloured and injured, by
the warmth and dirt of the hand of the operator.   Experience has demon-
strated that machines capable of cleaning four knives at a time, are by far
the most convenient and expeditious; the rapidity and ease of the operation
more than compensating for the employment of a machine capable of
cleaning a larger quantity.

In addition to the varied apparatus and machines above mentioned,
Mr. Masters exhibits an extensive series of domestic and culinary apparatus,
suited to the every day wants and requirements of all classes of the community, and in which elegance, economy, and utility are combined.

AGRICULTURE. AGRICULTURAL PRODUCTS. AGRICULTURAL IMPLEMENTS.

Agriculture.   Produits d'Agriculture.   Instruments d'Agriculture.
Ackerbau.   Landwirtschaftliche Producte.   Landwirtschaftliche Werkzeuge.

THE improved system of cultivation of the land, which has been introduced during the last thirty or forty years, has been attended with a greater degree of success, and added more to the agricultural resources of the kingdom, than many persons suppose. If we refer to the period between 1801 and 1810, we find, that whilst the amount of foreign wheat imported, sufficed to feed 600,946 of the population, at the rate of eight bushels per annum for each person, the remaining 11,168,779 were supplied from the produce of our own soil. In the period 1841 to 1844, although the increased quantity of foreign corn imported sufficed to feed 1,901,495 persons, yet such had been the improvements made in the cultivation of the soil, that the remainder of the population, 17,077,469 individuals, were fed with home-grown wheat; and although the quantity of wheat imported during the last two years has been sufficient to supply the wants of 4,000,000 people, at the same rate of consumption, yet 16,000,000 would even, on this calculation, receive their supply from home-grown wheat. It would, however, be absurd to suppose, that the productive power of the soil has diminished since 1844. A greater amount of other agricultural produce has been raised, to say nothing of the increasd consumption of wheat by the manufacturing classes, whose wages during the last two years have been higher than in previous years. We are therefore fully justified in stating, that the agricultural produce of Great Britain (for in these calculations we have omitted Ireland, which produces enough corn for her own wants) has risen considerably more than one-half during the last forty years. Such being the case, may we not look for still greatly increased results, from the resources of the chemical and mechanical science of the present day?

A careful inspection of the splendid collection of agricultural implements exhibited, will serve to show the visitor, that, in this department, we stand unrivalled, no other country venturing for a moment to compete with us in the mechanical appliances adapted to the improved tillage of the soil, and the economical preparation of farm produce for the market. The agricultural implement department, forms a complete exhibition of itself, and reflects the highest credit on the exhibitors. The mechanical productions of Crosskill, Wedlake, Ransome and May, Deane, Dray and Deane, and a host of others, show the great improvements which have of late years been made in farming instruments.

D

As it may not be uninteresting to the reader, to be informed of the amount of some of the agricultural produce imported into this country from abroad, we subjoin the following particulars relative to various articles entered for home consumption in 1850:—

VEGETABLE.

Agricultural produce.—Wheat 3,778,435 qrs. Barley, 1,042,801 qrs. Oats, 1,167,177 qrs. Rye, 94,078 qrs. Pease, 182,559 qrs. Beans, 449,493 qrs. Indian Corn, 1,286,281 qrs. Buckwheat, &c., 867 qrs. Wheaten flour, 3,858,332 cwts. Barley and oatmeal, 18,474 cwts. Potatoes, 67,444 tons. Arrow-root, 1,032,976 lbs. Cocoa, 3,103,926 lbs. Coffee, 31,226,840 lbs. Rice, 60,082,736 lbs. Ditto in husk, 37,154 qrs. Sago, 8,116,752 lbs. Sugar, 697,658,528 lbs. Tea, 51,178,215 lbs. Tobacco, 27,734,786 lbs. Treacle, 102,848,816 lbs.

Fruits, &c.—Apples, 323,644 bushels. Chestnuts, 74,546 bushels. Small nuts, 130,986 bushels. Walnuts, 44,406 bushels. Oranges and lemons, No. 173,795,915. Grapes of the value of £28,057. Almonds, 12,000 lbs. Currants, 45,403,456 lbs. Figs, 3,751,288 lbs. French plums and prunes, 2,021,264 lbs.

Spices.—Cassia, 97,539 lbs. Caraways, 620,928 lbs. Cinnamon, 28,448 lbs. Cloves, 159,955 lbs. Ginger, 1,442,560 lbs. Mace, 21,997 lbs. Nutmegs, 168,402 lbs. Pepper, 3,174,425 lbs. Pimento, 399,168 lbs.

Seeds.—Clover, 112,174 cwts. Linseed and flax seeds, 608,986 qrs. Rapeseed, 107,029 qrs. Tares, 27,298 qrs. Oil seed cakes, 65,055 tons.

Drugs.—Opium, 42,324 lbs. Rhubarb, about 60,000 lbs. Senna, 300,000 lbs. Jalap, 50,000 lbs. Sarsaparilla, 200,000 lbs. Castor oil, 1,300,000 lbs.

Timber for Building.—Colonial, 1,090,730 loads. Baltic, &c., 641,237 loads. Staves, 82,588 loads. *Hardwoods.*—Box, 860 tons. Cedar, 1,396 tons. Mahogany 30,000 tons. Rosewood, 3,600 tons.

ANIMAL.

For Food.—Bacon, 37,667,952 lbs. Beef, 15,166,368 lbs. Butter, 25,902,720 lbs. Cheese, 38,257,296 lbs. Hams, 1,305,584 lbs. Lard, 25,716,768 lbs. Pork, 23,659,664 lbs. Isinglass, 187,264 lbs. Anchovies, 141,052 lbs. Eggs, 105,780,540.

Live Animals.—Oxen and bulls, 28,951. Cows, 17,757. Calves, 19,754. Sheep, 137,646. Lambs, 5,852. Swine and hogs, 7,387.

For Manure, &c.—Bones, 27,183 tons. Guano, 116,926 tons.

The quantities of various vegetable and animal substances, imported and used in manufactures, are given under the respective heads of manufacture treated of in other parts of the Guide-Book.

MESSRS. DEANE, DRAY, and DEANE, of London-bridge, the well known agricultural implement makers, exhibit a variety of improved apparatus of various kinds, from which we select the following, as deserving of more especial mention :—

Patent Cess-pool and Tank Cleanser.—A most important adjunct to the sanitary movements of the present day, is obtained by the employment of this useful machine. The practical application of the principle on which its action is founded, (that of atmospheric pressure,) has long been tested and approved of as efficient, in the metropolis, and other large cities of France, where the regulations for the preservation of the public health, are more stringently and efficiently enforced, than in our own country. By the use of these machines, a cess-pool may be emptied in a short space of time, and without any inconvenience whatever; the cleanliness of the operation being such, that the machine may be used as well by day as by night. The insertion of the nozzel of the flexible hose into the material to be removed, and a few strokes of the air-pump attached to the upper part of the apparatus, being all that is required.

Iron Pig Trough.—One of the leading characteristics of the present age, is the application of iron to the construction of various articles of utility for which wood was formerly employed. Who would not prefer the use

of the above improved trough to that of the ordinary form, although constructed of iron? A whole family of grunters has here each his own separate trough, whilst, at the same time, he is taking his meals in common with the rest of his tribe.

Vegetable Washer.—This useful accompaniment to the farm-yard, is constructed with a rack and pinion, so that the cylinder enclosing the vegetables, may be raised out of the water, and emptied into a trough or barrow, with the greatest ease. This useful machine would be of use to the manufacturer of potatoe starch, and might be applied to other purposes of a similar kind.

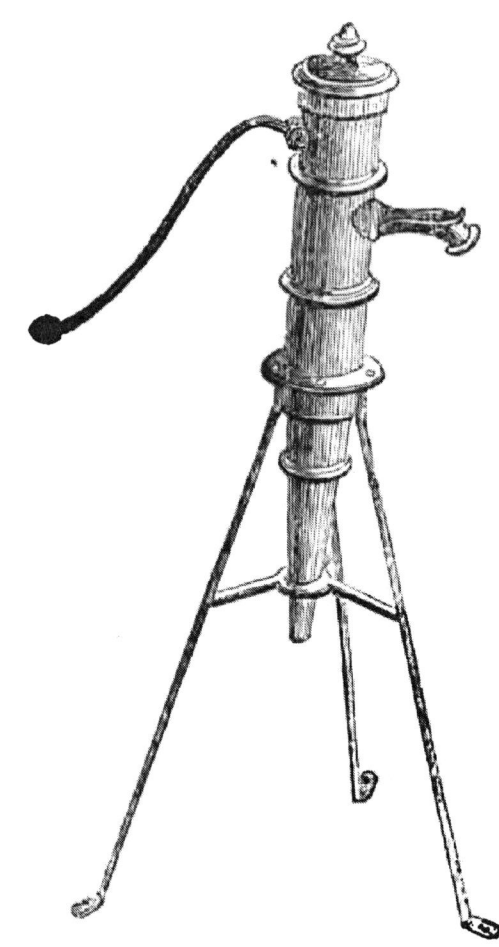

Wrought-iron Liquid Manure Pump.—It will be quite unnecessary, at the present day, even if we had ample room to spare, to dilate on the advantages derivable from the use of liquid manure to the agriculturist. The farmer must make use of all the appliances within his reach, in order to maintain his ground in these days of excessive competition, and, as the manufacturer adopts the most improved forms of machinery, so the farmer must adopt the most efficient implements and apparatus suited for agricultural uses. The wrought-iron liquid manure pump above figured, is one of the most handy and useful instruments a man can have upon his farm. It is so portable, that a boy can convey it from one part of the farm to another with the greatest ease. It will be found invaluable for emptying ditches, removing stagnant water, &c., and may be had of any height, so as to suit the various purposes to which its use is applicable.

Improved Corn Crusher.—Whilst the farmer is not neglectful of his land, and is endeavouring to obtain from it the greatest possible amount of produce, he must not neglect his horses, who, by their strength, render him that aid and assistance, in the transport of his manure, and his crops, without which he would be sorely inconvenienced. It is to the farmer's own interest to attend closely to the condition of his cattle, and, on this account, his attention to the nature of their food, and to the most efficient means of rendering that food capable of being assimilated by the system, and thus rendered nutritive, is of paramount importance. The old method of giving whole corn to horses is now almost exploded; the physiologist and the agriculturist, theory and practice, alike agreeing, that if the beans, oats, &c., be previously crushed, they are rendered more nutritious. A good corn crusher thus becomes a necessary addition to every stable, and its expense is soon repaid by the valuable results arising from its use.

Engine for Raising Water, and Improved Patent Force Pump.—Th engine, although one of most simple construction, is nevertheless admirably adapted for the purposes to which similar machines are applied. It is

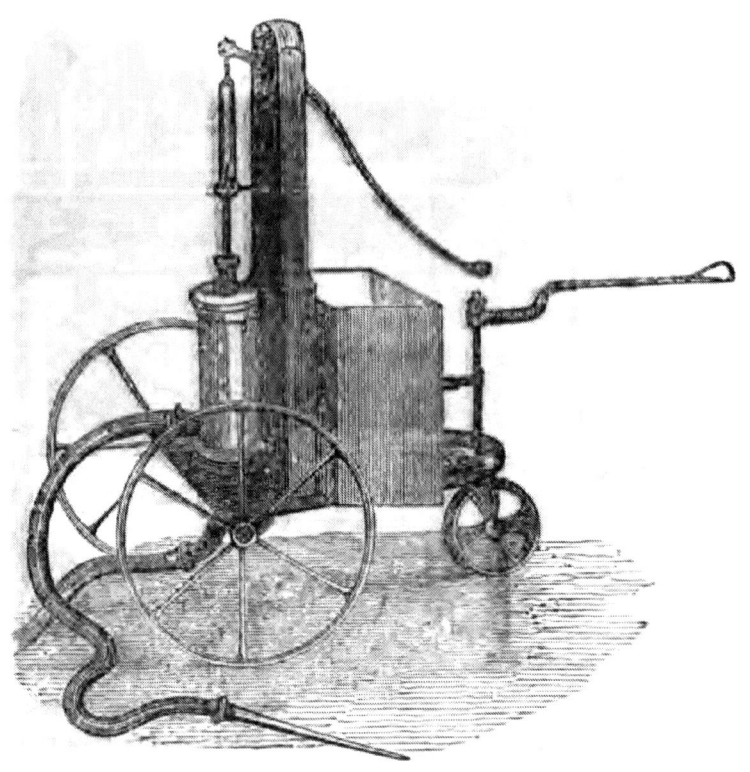

simple in construction, and easy to use. It may be employed for distributing liquid manure, and for watering lawns or gardens; at the same time, the principle can be adapted and applied as an improved patent force pump, the great advantages of which are, that whilst it is an excellent common house or yard pump, it also possesses the utility of the lift pump, for conveying water to the upper part of the house. This pump can also be used as a fire engine, throwing a column of water from forty to fifty feet high, by attaching a nozzel to the hose, which can be done in a minute. This engine would be found invaluable, for the purposes of exterminating vermin from fruit trees, &c. No mansion, garden, or farm premises, should be without one of those useful machines.

Improved Portable Smith's Forge.—The accompanying illustration, represents a smith's forge, which will be found to combine the great advantages of portability and efficiency. It is well adapted for the use of the farmer and the emigrant.

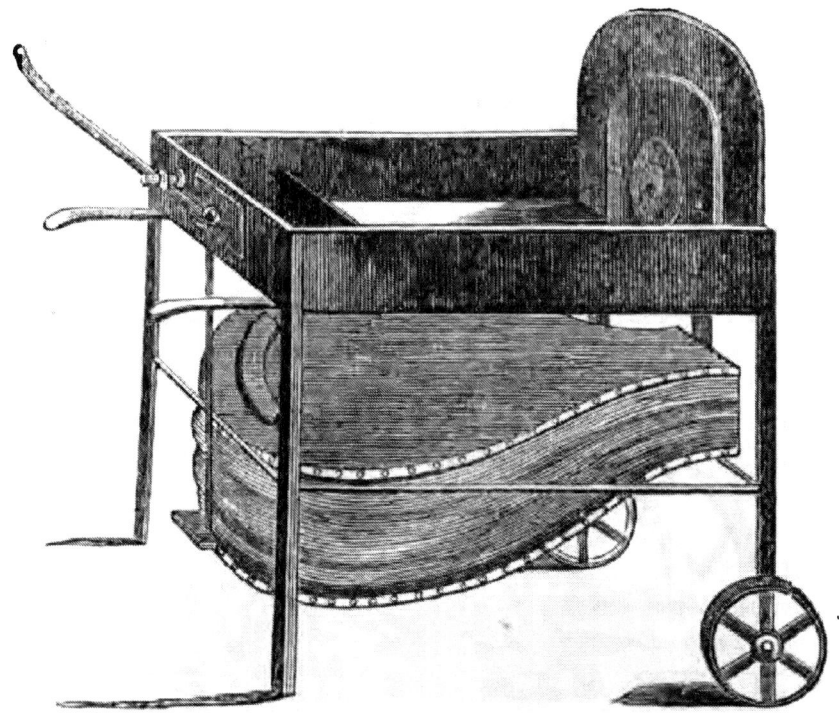

Double Weighing Machines.—
These machines are adapted either
for taking the article to be weighed
from the shoulders of a man, or for
weighing from a sack, truck, &c.
The same construction provides a
double scale for the weights also.
These machines are well adapted
for weighing farm produce, are correct, and very portable.

At the extensive depôt for agricultural instruments of Messrs.
Deane, Dray, and Deane, Swan-
yard, Thames-street, the intelli-
gent agricultural visitor will do well
to pass a day after visiting the
Exhibition, as he will there have the opportunity of examining more at
leisure, and of having fully explained to him, the advantages derivable
from the use of various implements of the most approved construction, as,
independently of being themselves extensive manufacturers, Messrs.
Deane and Co. are the representatives, in London, of most of the leading
agricultural implement makers in the provinces.

Improved Chaff Machine.—Messrs. Richmond and Chandler, of Salford, exhibit their chaff-cutter, for which a prize was awarded them at the Agricultural Meeting of the Liverpool and Manchester Society, in addition to five other prizes at the same meeting, the judges being three of the most practically scientific men that could have been selected, one of whom Mr. Amos, of the Royal Agricultural Society, then took the opportunity of introducing for the first time, the new system of dynamometrically testing machines and instruments. The chaff-cutting machine above represented, is self-feeding; the hay or straw is drawn under the knives by a pair of toothed roolers, of peculiar form, which grasp with great tenacity, the material to be cut, at the same time urging it forward, and preventing all liability to choke or lose the feed; by means of a lever, the mouth adjusts itself to any required feed. The chaff-machines are made of various sizes, suitable for land, water, or steam power, and will be found to be machines altogether of a very superior description, both in their construction and finish and calculated to take a much higher station, than the generality of agricultural machinery manufactured in Scotland.

PORTABLE STEAM ENGINE.

Machine à vapeur portative.   *Tragbare Dampfmaschine.*

THE application of steam power to agriculture, forms one of the triumphs of the present age. The portable steam engines constructed by Messrs. Lynch and Inglis, Garratt-road, Manchester, are admirably adapted for agricultural purposes, being easy of transport from one part of the farm to the other. These engines are also well suited for the use of contractors, merchants, and shopkeepers, requiring steam power in a small compass. They are of superior workmanship, are provided with metallic pistons, improved slide-valves, feed-pumps, and governors; they are simple in construction, efficient and economical in use, and may be put under the care of the most inexperienced person.

The travelling engine is fitted with an improved tubular boiler, safety-valve, water-gauge, &c. The prices of these engines are remarkably low.

PATENT SOFT METAL FOR THE BEARINGS OF MACHINERY, LOCOMOTIVES, &c.

Alliage doux pour coussinets de Machines, de Locomotives, et de Wagons.

Legirung zum Ueberzug der Stepsen in Maschinen, Eisenbahnwägen, &c.

One of the greatest benefits which have been introduced in the working of machinery, locomotives, &c., is the application of the soft metal bearings, invented by Messrs. Babbitt and Dewrance, as substitutes for the brass or gun-metal bearings, previously employed. In locomotive engines and railway carriages, the use of soft metal has been proved to augment the tractive power, by reducing the friction in the bearings; to increase the mileage or distance run, without the bearings requiring adjustment or repair, and to effect considerable economy in the oil or grease used. The soft metal bearings were first tried on the Great Western Railway in 1843, and the result was so satisfactory, that the whole of the Company's locomotive engines have been fitted with them. The great speed at which the passenger-trains travel, and the comparatively small size of the bearings in proportion to the weight they carry, are severe tests of the capability of the patent metal bearings, to resist heavy pressure at high velocities. An engine, the *Hercules*, travelled 73,000 miles without wear in her bearings. The increased distance which the engine can run with these improved bearings, as compared with those of gun-metal, without requiring repair, effects considerable saving in locomotive power and amount of stock. The patent metal bearings are made by casting a gun-metal shell, with a fillet of about an eighth-of-an-inch in depth,—this recess is lined with the soft metal.

The patent bearings of the *Kingfisher*, an engine on the Manchester and Liverpool line, were taken out for examination, after having run a distance of 60,272 miles; they were found to be in excellent condition, and not sensibly worn. By way of experiment, gun-metal bearings were tried, but they were found to heat and cut, and were replaced at once by the soft metal. The vantages of being able to travel more than four times the distance with the same bearings,—the high polish of the parts working in them decreasing the friction, and increasing the disposable power of the engines,—the facility of repair, when needful,—and the reduction both of time and cost in doing it, are great and manifest. An accurate account kept of the expenses attending the working of two engines, the one fitted with the soft-metal bearings, and the other with the gun-metal bearings, shows, that whilst the former had run 25,622 miles, the repairs, wages, and materials, cost £23 12s. 4d.; the latter, after running 22,298 miles, cost in repairs, wages, and materials, £158 10s. 5d.

The great economy in the oil required for lubrication, when the soft-metal bearings are used, is exemplified by the return made from the locomotive department of the Liverpool and Manchester railway, showing, that whilst 2,767 quarts of oil were required for the use of nine engines, running a distance of 125,475 miles, *prior* to using the soft-metal bearings, only 907 quarts of oil were required, by the same engines, running 98,273 miles, with the soft metal bearings, showing a difference, in favour of the latter, of 59 per cent.

The patent soft-metal bearings have also been applied to certain working parts of the engines, and propelling machinery, of her Majesty's steam yachts the *Fairy*, and *Victoria and Albert*. The successful application of these bearings is peculiarly remarkable, for before its introduction, the latter vessel could not proceed to sea without the crank-pins becoming so much heated by friction, as to render it imperative to stop the engines, when such stoppage was incompatible with the nature of the service ; whereas, since the use of the soft-metal, her Majesty's recent voyage to Scotland and back, was performed without any inconvenience.

Messrs. Squire and Co., of Barge Yard, Bucklersbury, are the proprietors and exhibitors of the patent soft metal bearings.

GAS METER.

Gazomètre. *Gasometer.*

In order to point out more clearly the advantages of this Patent Meter, over the old ones, it is necessary to explain the defects of the various kinds of apparatus now in use for measuring gas. In the ordinary wet meter with the revolving drum, the gas is admitted into separate chambers, formed by plates of metal, radiating from the centre, to the circumference of the drum, the measure of gas in each chamber being regulated by the height of the water-line : this being the case, it necessarily follows that every alteration in the quantity of water in the meter, gives a new measure of gas ; consequently the meter may be made to register more or less at pleasure.

In the dry meter, a partition, or diaphragm of leather or other flexible material is used for the measuring chamber ; the great defect of which is, the unequal, but unavoidable change of flexibility which takes place, to such an extent as to cause a false registration of from 10 to 20 per cent.

In Mead's patent meter, the gas is measured by a vibrating metal chamber, divided into two compartments. The gas on entering the meter passes into one of the compartments, immediately raising it until it has taken its measure, when the flow of gas is turned into the opposite compartment, and the measured gas is allowed to pass to the burners, the advantage of this arrangement being that the water-line may vary to a great extent, without in any way affecting the measure of gas ; in fact, as long as the meter will work, the measure is not affected by the water.

This meter is also exhibited by Messrs. Squire and Co.

CHRONOMETRIC GOVERNOR, FOR REGULATING THE SUPPLY OF POWER FROM STEAM ENGINES.

Gouverneur Chronomètrique pour règler la force motrice des Machines à Vapeur.
Chronometrischer Regulator zum reguliren der Kraft einer Dampfmaschine.

MESSRS. SQUIRE AND Co. are also the patentees of the chronometric governor, (invented by Messrs. Siemens, of Berlin), which has now been in constant use for a considerable time, for regulating the supply of power for grinding corn, and moving machinery of other kinds, and it is found to succeed perfectly in producing an instantaneous and automatic adjustment of the supply of power, without allowing any variation of speed; the result of which enables all manufacturers, dependant on regularity of the velocity for a maximum result, to attain a greater uniformity in, and increased quantity of, the manufactured article produced in a given time, without increasing the expenditure of power. This effect in grinding corn, amounts to an increase of 10 per cent.

These instruments may be applied to existing engines, water-wheels, &c., without interruption to their constant work, and at an expense much below the value of the advantages obtained.

APPARATUS FOR PREVENTING ACCIDENTS IN DESCENDING OR ASCENDING MINES.

Appareil de Sûreté, pour monter et descendre les Mines.

Apparat zur Verhinderhung von Unglucksfällen beim Befahren von Bergwerken.

———

OUR national importance is, in a great measure, dependent upon our immense mineral wealth, and our iron and coal may be considered as equal to two-thirds of the whole. The operation of mining for these valuable substances is, under the best circumstances, one of great difficulty, and always beset with dangers.

The Patent Safety Apparatus of the Messrs. Fourdrinier, has been most severely tested in several mines, and promises to afford an amount of safety to the miner which he has not hitherto enjoyed. The apparatus consists of a cage or basket, which can be employed in every way, precisely as any arrangement now in use. This is attached to guide rods or chains in the shaft, and upon the rope or chain being broken, arms, forming powerful levers, are liberated, and these are wedged most securely upon the guide rods. The apparatus has no chance of falling more than a few inches, after the rope or chain is broken. The stop is most perfect, and so free from any violent action, that no danger is to be apprehended from recoil. Another arrangement has been made, by which the casualties arising from being drawn over the pullies are entirely prevented. It must be understood, that this machine is perfectly self-acting, and that the greater the weights which may be in the cage, the tighter do the wedges hold upon the guide rods, in the event of any accident occuring.

Many of the most important coal-pits in the north are fitted with Messrs. Fourdrinier's valuable safety apparatus. The owners of mines are deeply indebted to the excellent apparatus of Mr. Fourdrinier, in saving, not only the lives of the workmen, but the property of such owners as have adopted it. The accident at Belmont colliery fully illustrated this position, wherein it was clearly shown that even one-half of the apparatus was sufficient to hold the cage, and thus prevent the damage which must have ensued, had there been no such apparatus on the cage.

PORTABLE FIRE-ENGINE.
Pompe à incendie Portative.   Tragbare Feuer Spritze.

THE fire and garden-engine above represented, made and exhibited by Messrs. Warner and Sons, of Jewin-crescent, London, is admirably adapted for the purposes for which it is constructed. It is provided with folding handles, for the convenience of passing through door-ways and narrow passages, and will deliver 30 gallons of water per minute to an altitude of 50 feet.

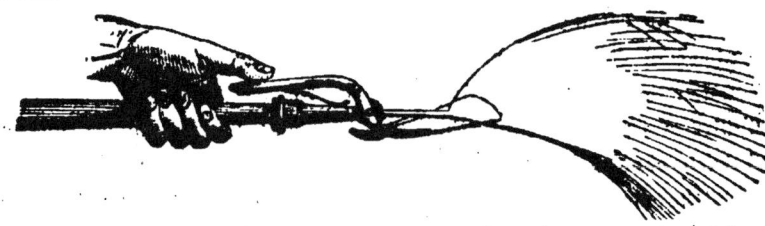

Water Spreader.—This apparatus forms part of the nose-pipe of garden-engines, and can be thrown in and out of action instantaneously; by its use, stoppage by means of dirt or leaves, which so often occur in "roses" and "fans," is rendered impossible. The spreader is also very efficacious when attached to the branch-pipe of fire-engines, and brought into use in cases when corn or haystacks are on fire. Every country fire-engine should be provided with one of these useful appendages.

CHECK INDICATOR.

Indicateur des Billets.   *Billet Anzeiger.*

THE numerous cases of fraud on the part of check-takers at theatres, and other places of public resort, where money is taken at the door, have led to the construction of the check-indicator, by the use of which machine, all possibility of fraud and embezzlement is prevented. The hollow tubes are filled with checks or counters, the number of which is known, and then locked; the money-taker moves the handle, and causes a check to fall out, which he delivers to the person from whom he receives payment. This check, in its passage out of the machine, turns the index of a dial, and thus registers the number delivered. These machines have been in use at the Theatre Royal, Drury-lane, for a considerable time, to the entire satisfaction of the manager. This machine should find a place at the entrance of all public exhibitions, institutions, steam-boat piers, and wherever money is taken at the door. Made and exhibited by Messrs. Warner and Sons.

ELECTRO-GALVANIC MACHINE.

Machine Electro-Galvanique. Electro-Galvanisch Maschine.

THE above engraving represents an instrument that is well deserving of additional notice; it is the electro-galvanic machine, the invention and manufacture of Messrs. Horne and Co., of Newgate-street, London. It possesses the long-desired power of transmitting, through any part of the patient's system, a uniform current of galvanism, and, at the same time, the mechanism of the machine admits of the nicest possible regulation, both of the quantity and intensity of the current When used with the chemico-mechanical battery, which stand beside it, invented by Alfred Smee, it forms the most elegant, as well as the most valuable arrangement for the administration of galvanism, that has ever been devised. There are other articles exhibited by the same manufacturers, that will repay inspection, as well from the skill displayed in the arrangements of the several parts, as from the exquisite beauty of the workmanship. The visitor ought not to omit to notice the ingenious apparatus for the detection of thieves, and for giving an alarm of fire, called Rutter's *patent electrical-indicator*, a sort of self-acting electric telegraph, which, when properly applied to a house, renders it impossible that a burglar should enter, or a fire break out, without immediate notice being given to the inmates. Two or three wires, not more costly, and less complicated in their arrangement, than the ordinary bell-wires of every house, give the ready means of communication from the remotest part of the building, which may be exposed to danger, and convey, in the clearest manner, the instant intelligence of " fire " or " thieves "; ringing an alarum, and pointing on a dial, the exact nature, and whereabout, of the danger. The invention is also applicable to ships, dockyards, warehouses, &c.

MANUFACTURE OF CHRONOMETERS AND WATCHES.

Fabrication de Chronomètres, Montres, &c.

Verfertigung von Chronometern und Uhren.

THE principal seats of the watch manufacture in England, are London, for watches of superior construction, chronometers, &c.; and Coventry and Liverpool for second class watches, mostly of silver, and of watches and works for exportation to the United States &c. In France, Paris is the reputed seat of this manufacture, but we have the word of M. Arago to the fact that but very few watches are really manufactured in Paris, Switzerland supplying by far the greater part of the watches sold in France. An immense number of works are made at Fontaine-melon and Beaucourt, in France, and exported to Switzerland, where they are polished and perfected by the Swiss artizan, and thence distributed to all parts of the globe. The principal seats of the Swiss manufacture, are the Cantons of Neufchatel and Geneva, in the mountainous districts of which the trade is carried on to a great extent, especially in the winter months, when the pursuits of agriculture are suspended. It is estimated that upwards of 100,000 watches, mostly with gold cases, are annually exported from Geneva, and as many as 140,000 from Neufchatel, seven-eights of which are in silver cases. The English watches are far more solid in construction and fitted for use than the Swiss watches, especially in countries where no good watch makers are to be found, as the Swiss watches require delicate treatment. English watches are therefore sold to those who can afford to give a good price, whilst the Swiss watches supply the class to whom a costly watch is inaccessible. The great advantage which the Swiss possess, in competition with the watch makers of England, is the low price at which they can produce the flat cylinder watches, which are so much in request. These watches are fitted with the horizontal escapement, the invention of an English clock-maker, Mr. Graham.

Whilst, however, the Swiss are enabled to furnish the markets of the world with watches of a moderate price, it is a well admitted fact that in all their attempts to make a really good watch, similar to those of the best London make, they are completely beaten in price by the English workman.

We would call the especial attention of the visitor to the following list of chronometers, watches, &c., exhibited by Mr. Charles Frodsham, successor to Arnold, Strand.

1. *Astronomical Clock*, with mercurial pendulum, Graham's dead-beat escapement.

2. *Marine Chronometers* on a new calibre, with Arnold and Earnshaw's detached escapement compensation balance of the ordinary kind, with Arnold's bar as an auxiliary compensation. This new calibre is based upon the plan of the diameter of a barrel, fuzee-wheel and extreme diameter of the balance being the same, namely, 1 in 5-10ths. The total weight of the compensation balance is 5 dwts., or as the contents of the barrel. Thus, if a barrel, 1 in. in diameter, by 8-10ths deep, will carry a balance weighing 20 grains, a barrel 1 in. in diameter, by 6-10ths deep, will carry a balance weighing 40 grains. The balance-spring is 15 inches long; the diameter $\frac{44}{100}$, the thickness of wire $\frac{1}{1000}$ by $\frac{1}{1000}$ broad, and the number of turns 10 to 12. The wheels (escape-wheel included) are each five times the diameter of their respective pinions, that is, the pinion upon which the wheel revolves. The fuzee-wheel 90 teeth, centre wheel 90, centre pinion 14, third wheel 80, third pinion 12, fourth wheel 80, fourth pinion 10, scape pinion 10, scape wheel 15.

3. *Specimens of Gold Pocket Chronometers, and Lever Watches*, reduced from the calibre of the Chronometer, with improved form of teeth of wheels and pinions, improved balance-springs, and mode of attaching the spring.

4. *The Double Rotary Escapement.*—This is a specimen of a new calibre movement, by which a powerful watch may be made in a flat case. This should have been the method adopted at the period when flat watches were first introduced, as it has all the advantages of a thick watch, that is, taking the contents of the barrel in diameter and depth as the basis of a power.

5. *Day of the Month Watch*, with lever escapement and double rollers. The calibre of this watch may be called more simple than the preceding one, only because it more closely resembles that which is daily made. The number of the teeth of the wheels is peculiar. The centre-wheel is much enlarged, with 160 teeth working in a pinion of 10, whilst the third wheel is diminished, which has 60 teeth working in a pinion of 10; the fourth wheel 63 teeth in a pinion of 7. Although this is a good working calibre for a superior watch, yet, if power is admitted to be a principle in watch-making, it is impossible to get the same depth of barrel in this watch, unless the calibre of No. 1 is used.

It may be here observed that in producing the foregoing calibres, all technical sizes have been rejected, and the common measurement of inches, tenths, hundredths, and thousandths adopted; so that from one calibre a watch of any other size may be made by the common rule of proportion.

6. *Specimen of Gold Lever Watches*, with the split-centre second's-hand movement. This watch being a perfect time-keeper, is capable of determining the precise time of any observation to a quarter of a second, by

means of an extra second's-hand, with which it is provided, and which in the ordinary state of the watch lies under the principal second's-hand, and travels with it. In taking an observation, the observer keeps his eye steadily fixed upon the object, and his finger in readiness to touch a spring, which allows the registering hand to fall simultaneously upon the face of the watch, where it may be allowed to remain upwards of forty seconds for reading off the time; which done, the finger is to be immediately removed in order to free the register, which instantly returns to its place ready for the next observation, without having in the least degree interfered with the correct performance of the watch.

7. *Specimen of Railway Watches.*

8. *Specimen of English Pinions for Astronomical Clocks.*

9. *Specimen of Carriage Clocks.*

10. *Specimen of Portable Chime Clock.*

11. *Specimen of Chronometer and Watch Movements.*

12. *Diagrams of Calibres of Chronometers and Watches.*

13. *Gauges for Admeasurement of Watch-work to the thousandth of an inch.*

14. *Specimens of Gold Watch Cases.*

15. *The New Calibre*, by means of which the manufacture of watches and chronometers is greatly improved and facilitated, and the expense considerably reduced.

To illustrate the chronometer calibre as applied to an ordinary watch, the annexed engraving of the balance and escape wheel, shows at once, the perfect freedom of all its parts, its simplicity, and its general application.

If a watchmaker were to try and cut down a good old watch, and attempt to make it a flat half-plate watch, that is, all the work flush with the upper plate, he would see at once the defect of the present calibre of the modern flat watch, with all its modern improvements,—or more properly, all its modern defects. Thus, take an Arnold pocket chronometer, preserving the same diameter of barrel and fuzee, which will be found to be of the largest dimension the same diameter of plate will allow, and reduce the same to a thin watch of exactly the same diameter, you will meet with one great obstacle, the largeness of the wheels; reduce them by the rule already given, take the diameter of the barrel for the diameter of the balance, place the three circles nearly in an equilateral triangle, only leaving room for the third wheel above, to pass freely between the barrel and the extreme diameter of the balance, the fourth wheel and escapement running under the balance, and with a little judgment and practice, you will have a beautiful calibre. Now this being done, let him compare it with a very modern watch of the same diameter of plates, (for superiority is only seen by comparison) and the modern watch will not bear the test; it will present a large diameter of plates with small power, much room lost, and though containing small works, these are not soundly free of each other, but subject to foul with the least dirt or giving way, whilst the chronometer calibre arrangement, with the same diameter of plates, will present large works, great power, and complete freedom of all its parts; thus, watches generally, constructed upon Mr. Frodsham's plan, even by very ordinary ability, would give much better results, than the present ordinary plan, carried out by skilful artists, as the diagram at sight will at once explain itself; accompained by its scale, it will need little detail, for the public will understand well the main features, sufficient to guide them in the purchase of a good watch. The watchmaker will by the diagram see as it were, a complete watch before him.

CHARLES FRODSHAM'S CHRONOMETER MODEL MOVEMENT,
New Series.

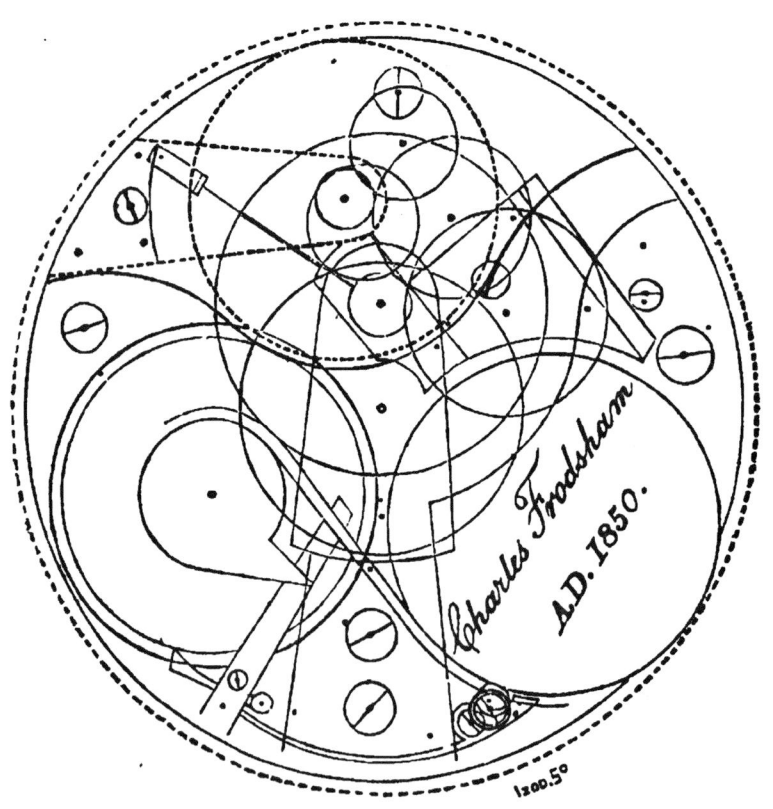

Mr. Charles Frodsham also exhibits the stages of manufacture of the chronometer compensation balance.

1st. Shows the rough steel cut from the bar.

2nd. Prepared for fuzing on the brass in the crucible, to obtain the compound laminæ. This is a very nice operation, and requires the steel to be prepared with the greatest truth.

3rd. The steel as drawn or taken from the crucible containing the melted brass.

4th. The process after fuzing on the brass.

5th. Its completion with adjusting weight, ready to apply to the chronometer, to be afterwards adjusted for temperature, an error amounting to almost 7 minutes per diem.

The number of watches made in this country, on an average of the last three years, is about 133,000, of which 23,000 are in gold cases, and 110,000 in silver. In addition to the watches exported from this country, which may be estimated as averaging about 20,000, a considerable number of sets of watch works without cases are annually exported to America. The reason of this is, that the duty on gold and silver watches, being an *ad valorem* one of 10 per cent, which with charges and other expenses, amounts to almost 20 per cent., the American merchant finds it cheaper to have the cases made at home, and therefore imports the works only from England. A considerable trade in watch works is carried on between Coventry and America, not less than 50,000 per annum, being at present exported. The value of the foreign watches imported into this country in 1850, was £97,245; and of clocks, £78,041; a duty of 10 per cent. being charged on importation. In the design and ornament of the latter, our foreign competitors excel, and the English market is consequently for the most part supplied from the continent.

The skill and precision of the English chronometer maker, may be rightly estimated, when we state that on a trial of nearly 500 chronometers, one of Mr Frodsham's make, varied but 0·57 during a period of 12 months Though our continental rivals may look on the Exhibition of 1851, as the arena in which the superiority of the French or English chronometer is to be decided, we feel no ground for alarm, when we know that our instruments find a market in France, notwithstanding an import duty of £21.

IMPROVED LAMPS FOR LIGHTHOUSES.

Lanternes de Phares perfectionnées.   Laternen für Leuchthürme.

On the value and importance of lighthouses, and a perfect mode of lighting, there cannot be two opinions; and when it is stated that the annual number of vessels wrecked amounts to 600, and that, independent of the vast sacrifice of human life, the loss of property from this source, exceeds a million per annum, it will be admitted that the subject of efficient lighting is one of extreme importance.

In the time of Charles II, large fires of coal on the summits of buildings, were the means made use of to give warning to the mariner. These were subsequently abandoned in favor of lamps placed before looking-glass reflectors, but from inefficiency in their construction and ventilation, resort was again had to the old system. The introduction of the justly celebrated Argand lamp, (the discovery of which was entirely accidental), forms, however, a most important era in the history of lighthouses; and although a vast number of modifications of the lamp have been proposed, none appears to possess any great advantage over that of Argand, his principle being adhered to in the construction of those in use at the present day, with this difference, that instead of using a single wick, two, three, or four, are now introduced. In order to obviate the charring of the wicks by the intense heat evolved, a certain pressure is maintained upon the oil, causing it to continually flow over the wicks.

As to the manner of reflecting the light thus obtained to considerable distances, our space does not allow us to enter into detail as to the various forms which have been given to reflectors, and the various materials of which they have been made; all, however, have been more or less defective, either from absorption of light, or from dispersing it in directions where it was useless. In 1811, Sir David Brewster discovered, after a series of experiments, that by cutting the ordinary convex or "bull's-eye" lens, in a series of steps, leaving a zone in the centre, the rays of light were projected horizontally in the direction required, and but a very trifling portion of the light was absorbed by the lens. This happy discovery, which was also made (simultaneously with Sir David) by the distinguished French optician, Fresnel, constitutes the basis of the high degree of excellence we have now attained in this respect. This principle of construction is termed the dioptric and catadioptric; the flame of the lamp is surrounded by a thick convex zone, or belt, of glass, above which is built in segments, a series of flat zones, progressively decreasing in size; the appearance of the flame presenting a solid pillar of light.

In the construction of these lamps, a large amount of practical skill,

acute judgment, and intricate knowledge of optics, are necessary, successfully to carry out the ideas of the philosopher; the happy combination of
these requirements, are evinced in the following improvements recently
effected in lighthouse lamps, by Messrs. Wilkins of London, and Letourneau
of Paris.

That appearance of light, called short eclipses, has been hitherto
obtained by the following arrangements:—An apparatus for a fixed light
being provided, composed of a central cylinder, and of two zones of catadioptric rings, forming a cupola and lower part, a certain number of lenses
are arranged at equal distances from each other, placed on an exterior
moveable frame, making its revolution around the apparatus in a given
period. These lenses, composed of vertical prisms, are of the same vertical
altitude as the cylinder, and the radius of their curves is in opposite
directions to those of the cylinder, in such a manner, that at their passage,
they converge into a parallel pencil of light, all the divergent rays emerging
horizontally from the cylinder, producing a brilliant effect, like that obtained
by the use of annular lenses at the revolving lighthouses.

New Arrangements.—The first improvement which we will describe,
has a special reference to the light, producing considerable economy in the
cost price, whilst the simplicity of the optical arrangements is by no means
its least recommendation. It consists, first, in completely dispensing
with the movable cylindrical lenses; secondly, it replaces these by one
single revolving cylinder, composed of annular lenses, and of lenses with
a fixed light introduced between them, the number of each varying
according to the succession of flashes to be produced in the period of
revolution.

The second improvement, of which already some applications that
have been made, serve to show the importance, consists in a new method of
arranging the revolving part. Experience has shown that the arrangement at present in use is very faulty; a short time is sufficient for the
action of the friction-rollers, revolving on two parallel planes, to produce by
a succession of cuttings, a sufficiently deep groove to destroy the regularity
of the rotatory movement. To obviate this great inconvenience, the
friction-rollers are so placed, that they are fixed on an iron axis, with
regulating screws, and traverse on bevilled surfaces.

The third improvement is the most important, the result being an
increase of the flashes in the revolving-lighthouses,—double what has
hitherto been obtained. By means of lenses of vertical prisms, placed in
the prolongations of the central annular prisms, the divergent rays emerging
from the catadioptric zones, are brought into a straight line, and lastly, a
coincidence of the flashes of the three lenses is obtained.

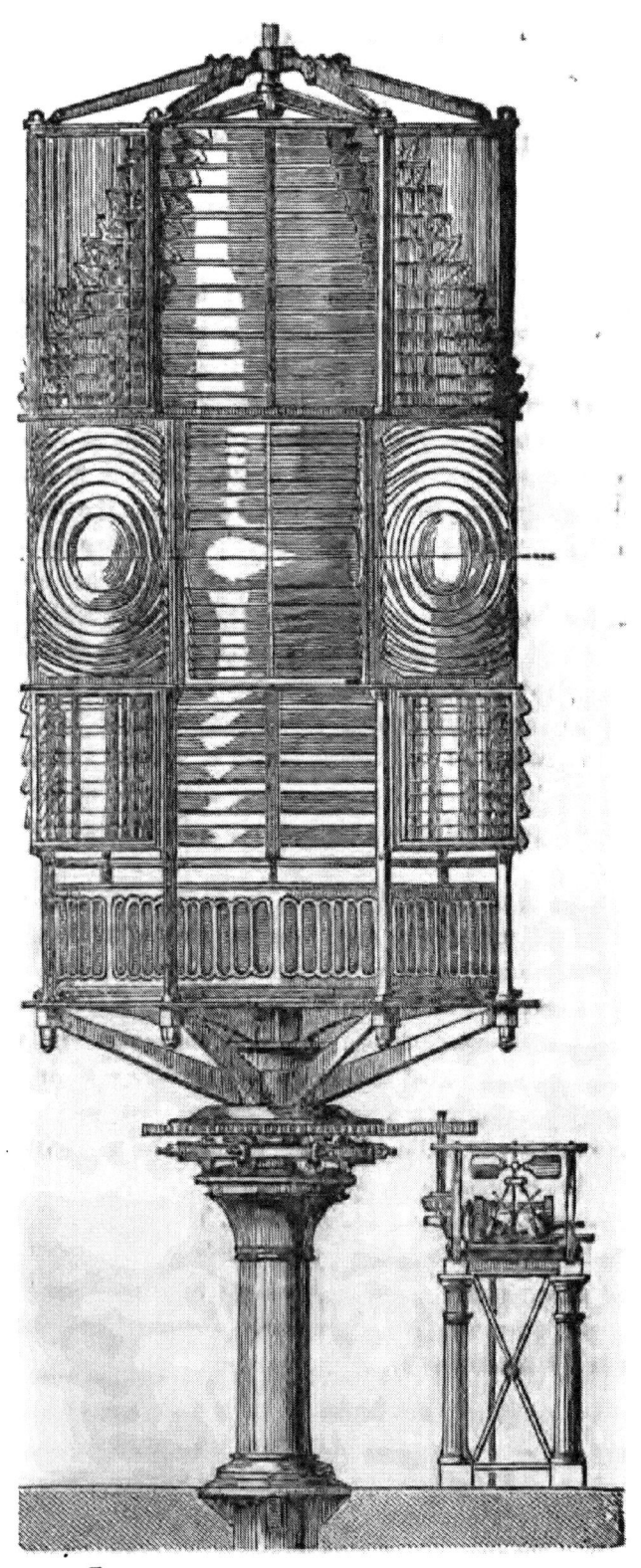

E

LAMPS FOR LIGHT-VESSELS.

HITHERTO, we have spoken of lights attached to fixed lighthouses, but as a variety of circumstances often occur to prevent the erection of lighthouses in such situations as are desirable, (as on the Goodwin Sands), it becomes necessary to employ other means of warning to the mariner on a dangerous coast. For this purpose "light vessels" are employed, with lantern and revolving apparatus attached to them. Mr. Wilkins has recently completed some improvements on the arrangement of these lights, possessing great advantages. The principal improvement consists, in constructing the machinery to work beneath the deck, instead of in the lantern as formerly. A vertical rod, working in metal bearings, is attached to the mast, with a large pinion fixed at the top of the rod, at the height to which it is necessary to hoist the lantern. The advantages of this arrangement are, that the lanterns can be made much lighter,—that the rolling of the vessel, caused by so great a weight at the mast head, is diminished,—and that the machinery, being more under control, and better protected from injury, works with far greater regularity and precision.

In the opinion of experienced persons, these improvements are most important; and the uninitiated may form an idea of their utility, by reflecting, that the situations in which light vessels are placed, are at all times difficult of access, and in stormy weather, when accidents are most likely to occur, quite unapproachable. There is also a vast benefit derived from the novel construction of the lamps and gimble work, which, by a movement, exactly coinciding with the motion of the vessel, causes a perfect level to be always maintained, and ensures the proper flow of oil to the burners, however rough the sea may be.

The engraving at page 73 represents Messrs. Wilkins and Letourneau's improvements in the lamps attached to fixed lighthouses; and that at p. 75, the improved arrangements of the lights fixed to "light vessels." The visitor to the exhibition will notice the perfect freedom from colour of the lenses of these lighthouse lamps.

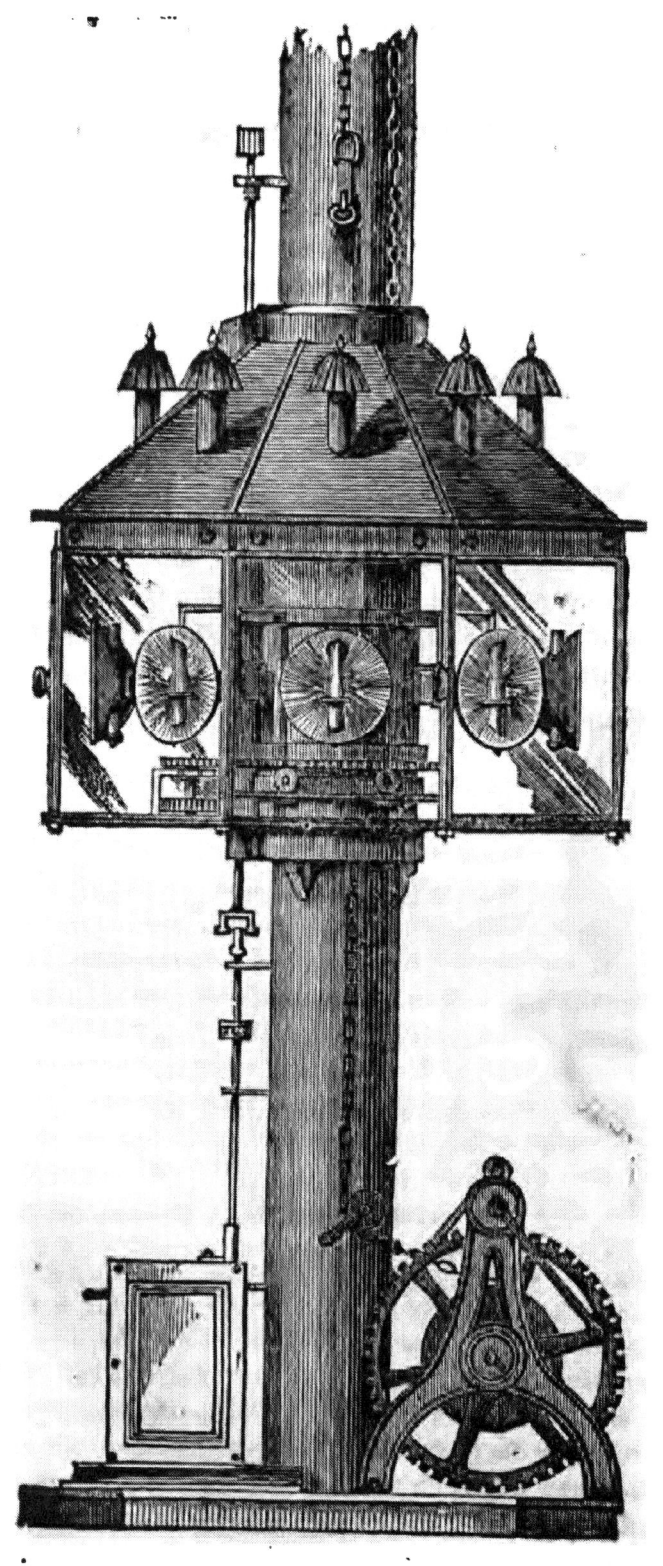

MANUFACTURE, PURIFICATION, AND COMBUSTION OF GAS.

Fabrication, Purification, et Combustion du Gaz.

Bereitung, Reinigung, und Brand des Gases.

WE now proceed to call the attention of the visitor to certain improvements connected with the use and purification of gas: and, when we state that not less than 6,000,000 tons of coal are annually consumed in this country in the manufacture of gas, and from £12,000,000 to £15,000,000 expended in its production, and that on an average, 9,000 feet of gas are produced from a ton of coal; some idea of the importance of the subject will be obtained. In London alone, 500,000 tons of coal are annually consumed, producing 4,500,000 feet of gas, and 500,000 chaldrons of coke. The length of gas mains in London is 1,600 miles.

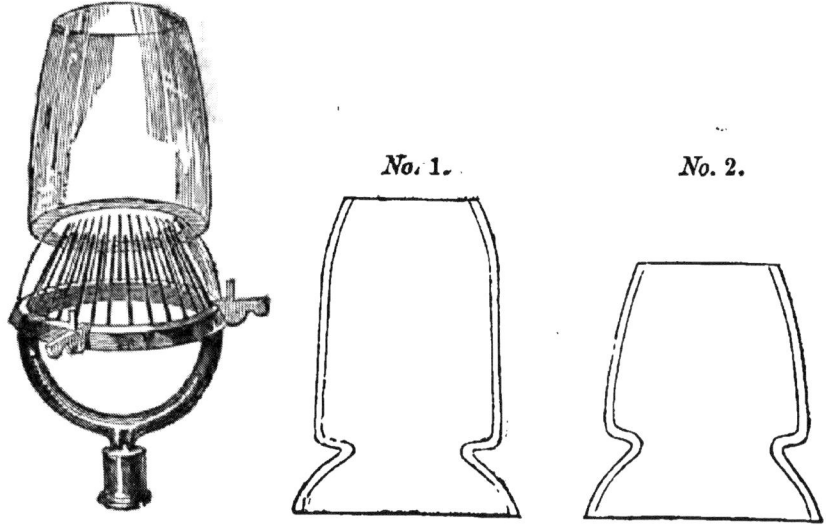

No. 1.   *No. 2.*

Mr. Leslie, of Conduit-street, has patented a gas burner, a representation of which is shown above. The gas flows through a circle of small tubes, each tube surrounded by the atmospheric current at the point where the gas is ignited and issues. In his researches on the evolution of light from gas, Mr. Leslie discovered that the *capacity* as well as the *shape* of the glass, materially influences the production of light; he, therefore, uses with the same burner, glasses varying in capacity, according to the desired quantity of light to be obtained; for example, the combustion chamber, No. 1, is applied when not more than three cubic feet of ordinary coal gas per hour are to be consumed ; No. 2 for four feet, and so on, increasing the capacity of the glass, or combustion chamber, if larger quantities are required through the same burner. By these regulations a flame is obtained, giving a greatly improved light ; but if the glasses be reversed, or if a larger quantity of gas than is due to the respective combustion chambers be admitted, a decrease in illuminating power is produced ; the great points to be obtained, being, the due regulation of the quantity of gas to be consumed, and the size of the combustion chamber corresponding to that quantity of gas.

Fig. 1.

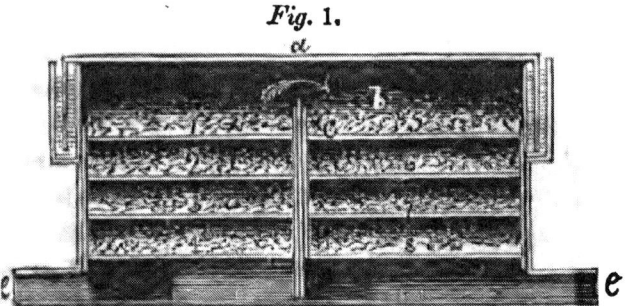

Of the injurious consequences to public health and property from the use of impure gas, there can be no question ; and in an economical point of view, it has been over and over again satisfactorily proved, that the illuminating power of gas increases in ratio with its purity ; hence the obvious utility of Mr. Leslie's patented arrangement, which ensures a supply of pure gas to the consumer. The compounds of sulphur and ammonia present in coal gas, and which have not been arrested by the purifying vessels at the respective works, are all registered by the meter to the consumer, who thus suffers both in health and in pocket. Mr. Leslie adapts a purifier to each house, through which the gas, as received from the street mains, has to pass in its way to the burners. Fig. 1, shows a section of the purifying apparatus. On either side of the centre division are placed four or more perforated trays, *b*, luted closely to the inner sides of the purifier ; each tray being three or more inches deep. These trays are filled with substances which absorb the more deleterious and non-illuminating products of coal gas ; the first, second, and third trays are filled with sulphate or chloride of copper, or both, in separate trays ; the fourth and fifth trays, with lime ; and the sixth, seventh, and eighth trays, with acetate of lead. Thus, the gas from the inlet from the street mains, must pass through the various substances in the eight trays, before it arrives at the outlet on its way to the burner.

Then, in order to ensure the delivery of the gas to the burners at a uniform pressure, Mr. Leslie devised his automaton gas-economizer. Fig. 2, shows a section of this useful apparatus; *h*, the inlet of gas; *g*, the only conducting tube to the outlet of gas; *f*, the slide to increase or decrease the aperture of the conducting tube of gas, according to the number of lights to be supplied; the stem of the slide works through a gas-tight stuffing-box, and has a pointer to indicate on a scale, the amount of opening, at *f*; *d*, represents an oil reservoir, as high as the dotted cross lines; *c*, dome to float in the oil reservoir, with cone at top. A small hole in the top cone is made to prevent the entire shutting off of the gas by violent or sudden pressure.

Fig. 2.

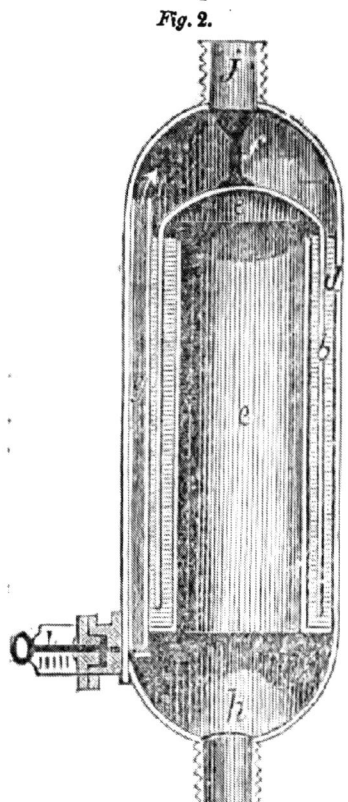

[In a recent report to the Government, Dr. Lyon Playfair estimates the combined advantages of Mr. Leslie's patent processes, at 71 per cent. as a minimum. At the General Post Office, in January, 1848, 228 of Leslie's patent copper tube burners, were substituted for 684 13-hole Argand burners; the new burners have been act·ing ever since, with great sanitary and economic advantage. The entire gas consumption of upwards of 600 Argand burners, has been saved. Upwards of 25,000,000 cubic feet of gas have passed through Mr. Leslie's purifying process, at the General Post Office, since October, 1847 ; the most moderate computation of the present saving, taking into consideration the enormous increase of business, and additional offices, will be 3,500,000 cubic feet of gas per annum, with the gratifying facts, that the offices already completed by Mr. Leslie, were never so well lighted, nor the atmosphere of the rooms so healthy and comfortable. The offices of the Commissioners of Her Majesty's Woods and Forests, the Ordnance and Foreign Offices, several of the leading banking houses, and large city firms, are enjoying the advantages of Mr. Leslie's patented improvements. At the Thames Tunnel, in which 143 of Leslie's burners are placed, 3,500,000 cubic feet of gas have passed the purifier, without the slightest stain being discovered, or the purifier having once been replenished. Mr. Mason, the engineer, reports that, whilst in

June, 1847, 120 of the old burners consumed 197,825 cubic feet of gas,—in June, 1849, 143 of Leslie's burners consumed only 177,700. Every fish-tail burner that was displaced by Leslie's 28 tube burner, caused a great increase of light, and, at the same time, a decrease of the gas consumed. The practical result being in strict accordance with the very able scientific report of Dr. Lyon Playfair, now before the Government,—that Leslie's burner, with the proper sized combustion chamber, and an equal quantity of gas, gave more than double the light that the bat's-wing or fish-tail burner could produce.

Mr. Leslie has also patented some improvements in the economy of fuel and ventilation, the practical results of which are very satisfactory. The fire-place in Mr. Leslie's grates is at the back, bottom and sides of fire-brick, with slight bars of iron to keep the coal from falling out, the only admission of air to support combustion being in front. The radiated heat passes along the floor of the room, instead of up the chimney; by this means the expenditure of fuel is reduced 50 per cent., and the ash remaining does not amount to quite 1½ per cent. of the coal consumed. These important principles above detailed, as to the great economy of fuel, is, by Mr. Leslie's patents, applied to all culinary and domestic uses.

GAS STOVE.

Poêle à Gaz.   Gas Ofen.

THE great reduction which has lately taken place in the price of gas, allows us to make use of it as fuel, for warming apartments, cooking, &c. The Registered Cylindrical Gas Stove, of Messrs. Deane, Dray, and Deane, affords a means of availing ourselves of the most cleanly, and least troublesome, as well as the cheapest, mode of cooking ever invented. For security against fire, it is also the safest. For warming churches, chapels,

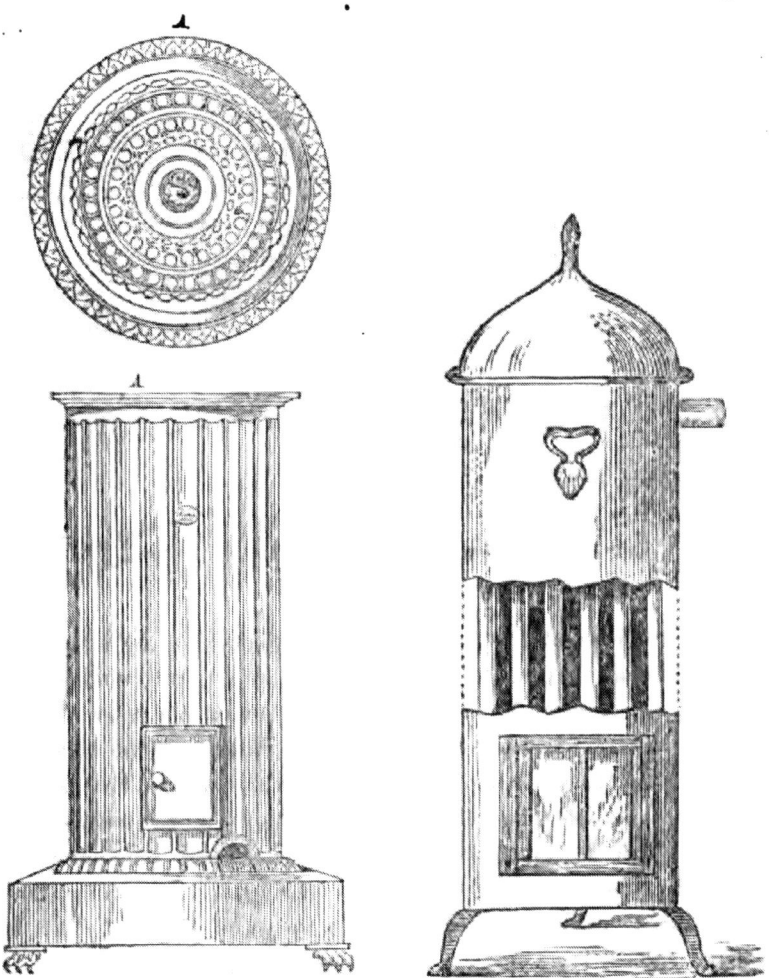

lecture-rooms, public institutions, offices, warehouses, libraries, nurseries, &c., indeed, wherever gas is, or can be introduced, this stove can be highly recommended, as the heat thrown out by it is genial and wholesome, and its economy (in consequence of the small quantity of gas necessary, and there being no waste of heat in cooking); is unquestionable. In this stove, the products of the gas consumed are not allowed to pass into the chamber so heated.

The *family stove for private houses*, is a very ingenious and complete apparatus, for performing all the various operations required in cookery. The oven, A, is fitted with moveable shelves, gridiron, dripping pan, hooks, &c., so that either roasting, baking, or broiling, may be carried on, as required. It has a damper-handle, to regulate the current of air passing through the apparatus; C, the chimney; D, the dripping pan; E, three boiling, stewing, or frying stoves, of different sizes. The top is made of raised ribs, for saucepans to slide upon. The opening, F, is for supplying air to boiling stoves; G, the gas-pipe, for supplying either burner of the stove, numbered 1, 2, 3, 4, by turning on the taps, H, opposite the respective numbers. Altogether, this is a most *convenient* stove, as well as cleanly and economical in its use.

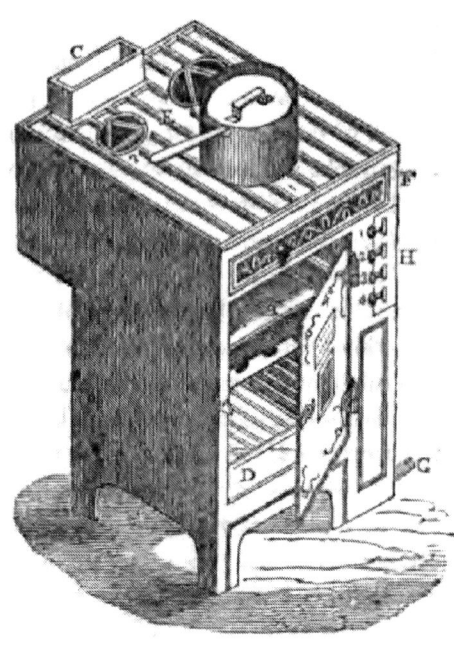

The sun gas-burner, is another invention of Messrs. Deane and Co., the use of which effects a saving of from 15 to 30 per cent. The small holes, which in the common Argand burners so soon corrode, or stop up, on account of the impurities existing in the gas, are, in this burner, entirely superseded, and a brilliant, shadowless, steady stream of light is obtained, free from deposit of any kind.

The commissioners having decided that no gas apparatus or stove shall be shown in actual operation at the Exhibition, we recommend our readers to visit Messrs. Deane and Co.'s establishment, King William-street, London Bridge, where these stoves may be seen daily in motion.

PYRO-PNEUMATIC STOVE.

Poële Pyro-pneumatique.   *Pyro-neumatisher Ofen.*

THE object of this invention is, to supply an *equable warmth*, and, at the same time, ensure *perfect ventilation*, whether in large public buildings, or in private apartments. Many improvements have, from time to time, been made in the various descriptions of stoves previously in use, but in each, and all of them, some serious objections remained, rendering their use often undesirable, and sometimes even positively injurious.

To our English tastes, there is something cheerless in the arrangement of *closed* fires, common to most of these stoves. The consumption of fuel is often very large; the circulation of air round the heated iron produces a pernicious change in the atmosphere, and the fire becomes intensely hot. Sometimes a disagreeable smell arises, from the combustion of the iron, or the sulphurous compounds in the coal, whilst the air is rendered too dry, and deleterious gases are formed, but not ignited, slowly escaping through the apertures of the stove into the apartment.

The inventor of the pyro-pneumatic stove, Mr. Pierce, of Jermyn-street, has, by a practical application of scientific knowledge, succeeded in overcoming these difficulties, and we now proceed to point out the admirable adaptation of Mr. Pierce's stove to all circumstances, by a succinct description of the principles on which it is constructed, which, while they merit praise for their simplicity, claim, especially on the ground of their sanitary effects, the highest approbation.

This stove is self-acting, and constantly maintains a supply of warm and wholesome air. It is constructed of *fire-lump*, having fluted sides of *pure anthracite fire-loam*, closely cemented together, and free from any admixture of iron. In the sides and back of the stove, are formed various passages and tubes, which are heated by the fire in the open grate. At the basement is an air-chamber, into which *fresh air*, from the external part of the building is admitted, and from which it ascends through the heated tubes and passages to the top of the stove, and thence escapes into the apartment, without coming in contact with any metallic substance. This warm air, as fast as it becomes deteriorated, is drawn back by the draught to feed the combustion. The sides of the stove, if, in a few years, they should become fractured or burnt, may easily be removed, and renewed; but this material, in the form of a brick, has been subjected, uninjured, to the heat of a cupola furnace. The back of the stove is hollow, through which the flame passes to a downward draught, the "lump" or "anthracite loam" still being the only material with which it comes in contact. The external casing of the stove, and, of course, the bars and bottom of the grate, are of metal; and as no injury from heat could occur, the external casing may be fitted up with glass, enamel, marble, or any other ornamental substance. The intensity of the heat can be increased at pleasure, but it is so equally distributed, that at the back or sides of the stove, the temperature is scarcely five degrees higher, than at any part of a well-constructed apartment, however large. It must be remembered, that the power of communicating heat, is thirty-three times less in clay or loam, than in iron; consequently, these masses of anthracite loam, being once heated, cool but slowly; and thus combustion is carried on very efficiently for many hours, with a mere

handful of fire in the grate, and under ordinary circumstances, warm moist air will continue to pass off into the apartment, at a temperature of 70 degrees; thus fully justifying the claim to *economy*, which the pyro-pneumatic stove justly assumes. In its plainest style, this stove is handsome in its form, and its capability, as before stated, of receiving any amount of ornamentation from non-metallic substances, allows the free exercise of taste in harmonizing and adapting its external appearance, to the edifice which it is designed to warm.

The smoke is carried downwards to the chimney-shaft, and the air of the room is so fresh and pure, that the most asthmatic person need not fear to breathe it. The quantity of fuel required, of course, varies with the size of the stove, and extent of the space to be warmed; but in the smallest size, it is found that 21 lbs. of coals are sufficient for the combustion of twelve hours, and that the largest size only requires 60 lbs. in the same space of time.

This is, indeed, a stove that warms and ventilates at the same time, and its manifest superiority cannot fail to recommend it for the church, the lecture-hall, the school-room, or the apartment of the invalid; indeed, wherever warmth and ventilation, both so important to *health*, are required.

Mr. Pierce has also invented a very neat and economical grate, for domestic use in cottages, lodges, alms-houses, &c.

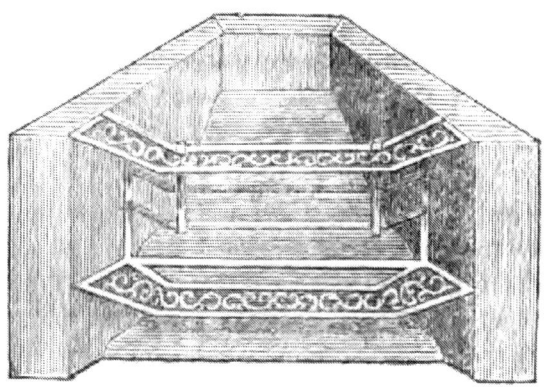

These grates are formed of the best and purest fire-clay, in one entire piece, and, therefore, require no fixing, but can be used in any room having a chimney. Fire-clay, as a material for grates, combines great strength and durability; and the construction of this grate unites comfort, economy, and general usefulness. It is fitted with strong iron bars, has capacious and safe hobs, which can be enlarged by the addition of a double top-bar, to hold pots, or other vessels, when boiling. It will consume any kind of fuel, either coals, coke, wood, or peat, and requires but a small quantity of either, yet producing a bright cheerful fire, without waste from ashes and cinders, and is, in all respects, admirably adapted for cooking.

By a very simple arrangement, and the admission of fresh air from the outside, this grate can be made to warm another room, either at the back, or a bed-room over, without any additional fire.

The original cost of these grates is extremely moderate.

HEAT AND LIGHT REFLECTING STOVE.

Poêle Réflecteur. *Reflectirender Ofen.*

THE continued and increasing demand for this unique stove, manifests its decided superiority for domestic purposes, such as dining, drawing, and breakfast rooms, libraries, &c. In large apartments, particularly if *long*, and the fireplace at one end, a single fire, however large, is often found quite insufficient for warming the room completely; and very often our feet suffering from cold, make us painfully conscious of the passage of currents of cold air across the floor. Johnson's stove is fitted up with a bright reflector, which completely surrounds the fire, and can be removed at pleasure. For a long room with the fireplace at one end, the parabolic reflector is best adapted, the light and heat from which are projected in parallel rays; while for a square or a long room, with the fire place at the side, the conical reflector is preferable, as it ensures a more extended diffusion of light and heat. In both cases the reflection takes place from

a comparatively cold surface, and therefore, the air is not deprived of its moisture, a point of great importance to health, no less than comfort. By the use of this reflector, a powerful warmth is felt at a considerable

distance from the fire, and *light* as well as heat diffused into every corner. To prove this, the stove may be tested by trying the effect of the fire without the aid of the reflector, when very little heat will be obtained at a certain distance from it; no more, indeed, than would be afforded by an ordinary fire in a grate of the same dimensions: the addition of the reflector, however, produces a powerful heat from the fire, which is felt at a considerable distance, rendering this stove pecularly applicable in the case of long rooms.

Much dust is avoided, as well as the unsightly appearance of ashes and cinders, the grate being so contrived, that the ashes fall at the back, into an ash-pan, placed out of sight, and which may be occasionally emptied, by drawing out the reflector; thus the constant advantage of a clean hearth is ensured. With regard to smoke, these stoves appear to answer perfectly, and to have cured even *smoky chimnies*. While these stoves afford a vast amount of heat, the temperature can be regulated at pleasure by a simple, but perfectly effective arrangement; and thorough ventilation is amply provided for. In all new inventions, economy is a great point in weighing their respective merits, and in this particular, the testimony of many individuals of the first respectability who have fairly tried them, must be considered as conclusive. They agree in stating, that Jobson's stove furnishes *increased* heat, with the saving of nearly *one-half* the fuel required in ordinary grates. Besides these advantages, the liability to fire is materially lessened, by the circumstance, that in setting this stove, every part of it is in contact with solid brickwork, and thus the accumulation of soot is prevented. The appearance of this stove is extremely elegant, and ornamental, and the form is peculiarly susceptible of embellishment and decoration. The price is, also, considering its numerous advantages, exceedingly moderate.

MANUFACTURE OF PORCELAIN AND EARTHENWARE.

Fabrication de Porcelaine et de Faïence.
Manufactur von Porcelain und Steingat.

THIS interesting branch of the manufactures of our country, which in the hands of Wedgwood, Copeland, &c., has acquired so much importance, is for the most part located in that part of South Staffordshire, to which the appropriate name of " Potteries " has been given. To attempt to give even an outline of the various departments of this branch of industry, from plain ware, to the finest porcelain, would take up more space than our limits will allow; suffice it therefore for us first to state, that the following raw materials are employed in the manufacture of the various kinds of earthenware and china, viz. : plastic clay, china clay or kaolin, granite or Cornish stone, burnt bones, chalk flints, steatite or soap-stone ; all these ingredients are ground, suspended in water, and united in various proportions in the form of a paste, with a certain admixture of what is termed " frit," composed of Cornish stone, flint, soda, borax, and oxide of tin. A lump of this paste having been brought to the workman in the foreground of the annexed engraving, of sufficient size to form a vase, he has placed it upon a plaster support, which comes to the top of the axle of the lathe, and he is now in the act of what is termed " throwing or " turning," working with his foot and hands at the same time. By his side is an apron for catching the " slip " thrown off in the operation. The other workman is employed in finishing the piece according to the model vase before him, which is the pattern of the one in progress. The vase is then dried in the shade, and afterwards " fired " in the oven or kiln ; where it becomes what is called " biscuit " ware, and is now sufficiently porous to receive the " glaze," composed of felspar, gypsum, &c.; this glaze being mixed with water, the biscuit absorbs the moisture, and the glaze remains attached to its surface. The vase is then placed in the furnace or kiln, and at the end of a certain time is taken out ready for use. The materials employed, and the operations following, vary according to the peculiar character of the ware to be obtained.

Printing on earthenware is thus performed: a printing ink composed of the desired colour, such as cobalt blue, manganese black, chrome green, or any other that will stand the action of the furnace, is mixed with

linseed oil varnish, and a copper-plate impression is printed with this ink, upon the paper in the usual manner. This copper-plate print is made to adhere with the printed surface towards the earthenware, and the article to which it is adapted, is then dipped into water. By this means, the paper and the adhesive matter is softened, and can be brushed away, while the coloured varnish which is not affected by water, remains as a picture upon the biscuit, and the varnish being destroyed by heat or hardening, it is glazed and the design burnt in.

Messrs. John Ridgway and Co., of Cauldon Place, in the Staffordshire Potteries, exhibit the undermentioned unrivalled specimens of ceramic art:—

Porcelain Table Services.—Specimens of a splendid coral and gold suite, with the united arms of the Ricardo and Duff families, exquisitely painted; also of a second suite in marone, buff, and gold; and of a third, with wild flowers and gold, in the best style of Dresden. The shapes,—all novel,—combining the style of silver, with the taste of china.

In addition, twenty-four or more pattern plates, consisting of a beautiful variety of forms, colours, and finish, some of them truly magnificent; and particularly one, the border bright and chased gold,—the centre, the arms of Lord Ward, superbly painted.

Porcelain Desserts.—Specimens of one service in azure and gold, with select views from all countries; of a second in coral, with watteau centre and gold; of a third in mazarine blue, fruit, and gold; and of a fourth, with exquisite groups of plants and gold. Besides these, thirty-six dessert plates, of every possible character and decoration, and among the rest, a square form of a most tasteful description, worthy of being set in frames, for a drawing room.

Porcelain Tea and Breakfast Services.—A part of several tea suites, given in small groups, of breakfast suites in larger and smaller ones, so as to show the shapes in great perfection. Besides these, there is a large assortment of single patterns, of splendid forms and decorations, which must be seen before any idea can be formed of their variety and elegance.

Porcelain Candlesticks.—This is a little assemblage of gems, and will prove very attractive.

Fine Earthenware.—Specimens of table services, of the newest shapes and of superior fabric, in colours and gold; of dessert services, the same; and also of toilet services. It is unnecessary to describe this tasteful variety, but the polish of the glaze, and the solidity of the texture, will deserve particular attention.

Conservatory Fountains, large and small.—These magnificent and unique articles are adapted to conservatories and lawns; they are perfectly novel, and beautifully applicable to the purpose. The finishing is both highly decorative, and particularly simple, so as to suit all classes; the articles are, moreover, exceedingly cleanly and durable.

Domestic Fountain Basons.—These also are perfectly new, and their elegance only to be equalled by their utility and adaptation to domestic comfort and convenience,—as such, we recommend them to special attention.

Graduated Garden Pots.—Of a peculiar construction, for keeping the soil more or less moist, without coming in contact with the water. The shapes, colours, and models, will speak for themselves.

Pottery Stone Taps.—These have been manufactured for some years, with an increasing sale, and when it is known that they are proof against acids, and extremely durable, they will need no other recommendation.

Sanitary Vessels.—At the instruction of the Board of Health, Messrs. R. and Co. have prepared a series of these vessels, altogether novel in their construction; new also as an application of pottery, and calculated to confer a most important service on all classes, but especially on the labouring millions, for their comfort and health.

Pottery Ovens, for cottage accommodation; and also specimens of *Hollow Bricks*, prepared for external and internal service; as also for ceilings and floors.

France possesses extensive manufactories of earthenware at Bordeaux, Montereau, Creil, Arboras, Toulouse, &c., which export to the amount of £28,000 per annum. The porcelains of Sèvres, Limoges, St. Yrieux, &c., are exported to the annual amount of £200,000.

The quantity of earthenware, of British manufacture, exported in 1850, was 76,952,735 pieces, of the value of £999,354. The United States takes nearly one-half of the quantity exported, Brazil, the East Indies, Holland, and the Hanseatic Powers, being our next best customers.

MANUFACTURE OF GLASS.

Fabrication de Verres et Glaces.   *Glass Manufactur.*

———

EMBROIDERED GLASS,—GLASS SHADES.

MANY circumstances contribute to render glass one of the most curious and interesting of manufactured substances. Although perfectly transparent itself, not one of the materials, of which it is made, partakes of that quality; exceedingly brittle while cold, it becomes, by the application of heat, so remarkably flexible and tenacious, as to become convertible into every form that fancy may dictate, or convenience suggest. The manufacture of glass has long been a very considerable branch of industry in this kingdom, and had it not been for the oppressive *incubus* of the excise, it would, many years since, have attained that eminence, which, since its emancipation from the fiscal regulations of the State, it is now rapidly acquiring. For the manufacture of glass, in all its useful and ornamental branches, this country possesses indigenous resources superior to those of every other, in its stores of fuel, and vitrifiable materials of every kind; yet, even at the present day, our list of imports show, that we are still indebted to foreign countries for some portion of the glass we consume.

There are five different and distinct qualities of glass manufactured for domestic purposes, viz., flint glass or crystal; crown or sheet glass; broad or common window glass; bottle or common green glass; and plate glass. In addition to these, there is glass manufactured for optical purposes, and glass of various colours. Each of these varieties contain, in common with the others, two ingredients, which indeed are essential to their formation: these are silica and an alkali. For the silica, certain kinds of sea-sand are employed, the preference being given to that obtained from Lynn, in Norfolk, and Alum Bay, in the Isle of Wight. The alkali used is either potash or soda, chiefly the latter. The ingredients which vary, not only for each kind of glass, but often for the same kinds, made by different houses, are melted in pots made of Stourbridge clay, and the vitrified mass thus obtained, is next treated according to the particular purpose to which it is to be applied. Our limits will not allow of our entering into any detailed account of the manufacture of these various kinds. of glass. The specimens of glass, in various stages of the manufacture, exhibited by Mr. Hartley, of Sunderland, also renders this unnecessary. To these specimens we would call the especial attention of the visitor.

For specimens of flint glass, we must direct the attention of the visitor to the exquisitely rich and magnificent displays of Mr. Apsley Pellatt, of London, and Messrs. Osler, of Birmingham. Flint glass, so called because flint was first employed in the manufacture as the source of the silica, owes its distinguishing characteristic to the presence of lead. The discovery of this lead glass is of English origin; it is peculiarly adapted for articles of luxury, such as chandeliers, goblets, decanters, &c.; from the ease with which it is cut or ground; from its brilliant lustre, high refracting power, and perfect freedom from colour, so that the term crystal glass has been applied to it. Flint glass is either formed by simple blowing with the pipe, by blowing in iron or brass moulds, or by moulds alone; in every case, the form can be improved,—as is usually done,—by subsequent grinding, &c. Although moulded glass can never be compared with cut glass, yet the use of the mould, as a preparatory step to grinding, is of great advantage to the grinder, as the vessel acquires a perfectly regular form, and although in a crude state, presents all the prominent and receding facets, to be perfected at the lathe.

The grinding or cutting of glass is effected by means of discs of iron, sandstone, or copper, which revolve in a kind of lathe: their edges, which are sharp, regular, or rounded, being supplied with sand, for *rough* grinding, and with emery for *fine* grinding. Similar discs of tin, wood, or cork, used with pumice-stone, or colcothar, are employed for polishing the glass.

Plate glass is obtained by casting, or running the melted mass on cast-iron slabs of the requird length. The rough plates of glass thus obtained, are then polished, by rubbing them with oxide of iron, or colcothar. The amount of time and labour expended during the polishing of plate glass, may be estimated from the fact, that the plates are by it reduced one-third, or even sometimes one-half in thickness.

Coloured glass is obtained by the addition of various metallic oxides to the usual ingredients; thus, the oxides of silver, antimony, and uranium are employed, to give a yellow colour; oxide of iron, and sub-oxide of copper, for red; oxide of copper, and oxide of chrome, for green; oxide of gold, for ruby; oxide of cobalt, for blue, &c.

"The removal of the oppressive excise laws, has given a most extraordinary stimulus to the glass trade, and numberless applications of it to useful purposes will be seen at the exhibition.

In 1801, with a population of 16,000,000, the quantity of glass used was 325,529 cwts.; and in 1833, with a population of 25,000,000, the quantity used was not more than 363,468 cwts.; an increase of less than one-eighth, whilst the population has increased one-half. The pernicious effects of the excise regulations checked the progress of invention and improvement, and a manufacturer dared not obtain superior excellence in any branch of the trade, lest his productions should be taxed with a higher rate of duty on account of their assimilating with a superior class of goods. Plate glass has now become, not a mere luxury, but almost an absolute necessity in domestic use. Its extreme cheapness compared with its former dearness, provoked greatly by French rivalry, has been the means of introducing it into dwellings, where formerly its appearance would have been deemed extravagance, and few shops of any pretensions are now opened without handsome plate-glass fronts. The "Crystal Palace" itself is a monument of the beneficial effects which have resulted from the repeal of the glass duty, which, on the quantity used in this structure, would have amounted to a prohibition. Not only in a commercial, but also in a moral point of view, the repeal of the excise duty has been attended with beneficial results, inasmuch as it has put a stop to the illicit manufacture of flint glass, which, previous to the removal of the duty, prevailed to a considerable extent.

There were imported in 1850, 21,048 cwts. of window-glass, not exceeding 1-9th of an inch thick, and shades and cylinders, of which 9,406 cwts. were entered for home consumption, and 11,604 cwts. re-exported; 122,391 square feet of glass, exceeding 1-9th of an inch thick, and silvered or polished glass, of whatever thickness, of which 89,522 feet were entered for home consumption, and 32,408 feet re-exported. Also 95,439 lbs. of white flint glass goods (except bottles) not cut, engraved, or otherwise ornamented, of which 23,987 lbs. were entered for home consumption, and 69,859 lbs. re-exported; and 884,998 lbs. of flint cut glass, flint coloured glass, and fancy ornamental glass, of which 663,904 lbs. were entered for home consumption, and 187,202 lbs. re-exported.

The glass manufactures of British and Irish produce, exported in 1850, were—24,063 cwts. of flint glass, of the value of £106,191; 15,518 cwts. of window glass, of the value of £20,079; 297,033 cwts. of bottles, green or common, of the value of £168,759; and plate glass of the value of £18,317.

This brings us to notice Mr. Kidd's "New Process for Embroidering and Silvering Flat Surfaces in Glass," which is adapted to articles of use, ornament, and furniture generally; and affords a striking instance of what may be done by long-continued perseverance, constantly directed to one great object. This very beautiful invention is avowedly applicable to FLAT surfaces in glass only, and not to hollow bodies,—as vases, goblets, &c. It not only differs from, but far excels in elegance and chasteness of design, all other known methods of ornamenting glass.

The elaborately-beautiful specimens exhibited by Mr. Kidd, at the "World's Great Fair," present the most exquisite designs,—and every pattern, although commenced, continued, and perfected on the under side of

the glass, stands out, when finished, in the highest possible relief; appearing, in fact, as if embroidered *on* the glass. Notwithstanding the hardness of the substance worked upon, these ornamental patterns have all the exquisite finish of the most elaborate pencil drawing,—from the finest tendril of a leaf, to the most minute petal of a flower. The elegance of the borders, embroidered on the girandoles, cannot be surpassed. The grouping

of the flowers, and the truth of the drawing, no less demand our admiration, than the delicate precision with with every detail of petal, leaf, and tendril is brought out in dead and burnished silver; whilst the happy introduction of animated objects in the most natural positions, gives a new charm to these exquisite wreaths. Amongst many artistical designs, our space only allows us to particularize one more instance,—it is that of a superb wreath, formed entirely of the "lily of the valley." In this, the bells of the lily only are in burnished silver, and the effect is at once brilliant, elegant, and chaste. Many attempts have been vainly made, both by the Venetians, and our own countrymen, to accomplish what has now been done. Of *modern* specimens, those shown at the Paris "Exposition," of 1849, were simply pieces of glass, commonly engraved, or etched with fluoric acid, and imperfectly silvered with mercury; their lustre, if such it may be called, is extremely short lived. The process by which hollow bodies are "silvered," is a purely chemical one, and therefore liable to injury, from exposure to damp, heat, or light. In Mr. Kidd's process, the magical effect of the ornamented wreaths, &c., is produced by means of a lathe, and an immense number of minute edged-wheels, with which these pencil-like touches are actually *worked into* the glass. The perfection and admirable adaptation of the tools, to produce the minutest tracery on the glass, and the rich appearance of the finished work, are indeed surprising. The *artist-workman* having with his many wheels, and wonderful skill of hand, produced upon the glass the required pattern, in readiness for the silver, the "embroidery," (as it is most expressively and appropriately termed), is next coated with a peculiar "preparation," the secret of the inventor, and not known even to the workmen who use it. This preparation causes the close and firm adherence of the silver; and it has also the remarkable property of rendering the silver more white; thus bringing out the patterns in still bolder relief by time. The "embroidery" being thus prepared, the silvering is *impressed*, not deposited by any chemical action, upon the engraved pattern. A peculiar process is also used in "fixing" the silver, whereby is obtained an imperishable metallic lustre, causing the artist's designs to be thrown out in the boldest relief.

Mr. Kidd's contributions to the "Great Exhibition," are both numerous and varied, and they will open a wide field for architects and artizans. The applications of the process are almost unlimited,—and for decorative purposes, it must come into universal demand.

Lastly, under this manufacture, we would call attention to the display of Glass Shades exhibited by Messrs. Hetley and Co., of Soho Square.

There is something very singular in the name which has been applied to these elegant and useful forms of glass, both in France, where they were originally invented, and in England, where they have now become comparatively common. The French name first given to them, was *cylindres de verre*, as they were first made in a cylindrical form; but as they were afterwards made oval and square, the strange jumble of words, "oval cylinders" and "square cylinders" then came into use; the English name "shade" is not less anomalous; for nothing can less resemble a shade, than a glass cylinder. Some years since, we imported all our glass shades from France, now most of those sold in this country are made at Birmingham. Considerable difficulty was at first experienced in cutting these shades of the required accuracy. Several extremely elegant mechanical processes, have, however, been successfully adopted, and the cutting of the shade by means of the diamond so accurately accomplished, that it is made to stand perfectly even on a level surface, every particle of dust and smoke being excluded by the accuracy of the cutting. The shade being fixed exactly upright, the cutting is performed as follows:—a small but heavy metallic case, moulded on three spherical castors, carries an upright rod, at the extremity of which, the cutting diamond is fixed in a horizontal position. A second rod, terminating in two small wheels, covered with cork, which come in juxta-position with the diamond, turns upon a pivot connected with the principle stem of the instrument, and the wheels are pressed towards the diamond, by means of a spring acting between the rods below the pivot: the shade, when finally adjusted in its position, being made steady by a small elastic rod, coming from one of the upright grooves, is ready to be cut, and for that purpose, the instrument in which the diamond is inserted, is brought underneath it, and the edge of the glass brought between the diamond and the wheels. By the contact thus produced, and the heavy base of the cutting instrument being carried round the shade, the diamond makes a clean cut, and a strip of glass is taken from the shade, which then stands quite even on the section. Glass shades form quite a leading object in the "Crystal Palace;" insomuch so, that it was scarcely necessary to have allotted any particular space for their exhibition. In addition to the vast numbers supplied by them to the various exhibitors, Messrs. Hetley and Co. exhibit specimens of glass shades of every size, remarkable for their clearness and transparency.

WOOLLEN MANUFACTURE.

Fabrication de laine.   *Wollen Manufactur.*

This, which for so long a period was the staple manufacture of the kingdom, and which in the time of the Stuarts formed one-half of the total value of the exports of the kingdom, has for some years past occupied but a second place in the list of exports; the rapid growth and progress of the cotton trade, having obtained for that comparatively new branch of manufacture, the proud position of heading the list of British produce, exported to foreign countries.

In the time of Charles II, when the whole exports of the kingdom did not exceed £2,000,000, the woollen manufactures figured in the list for £900,000. In the reign of William III, when the exports had risen to £7,000,000, the woollen manufactures contributed £3,000,000; the exports gradually increased to £6,876,939 in 1799, since which time they have undergone many fluctuations, being in 1833, £6,539,731; in 1849, £8,452,946; and finally attaining in 1850, the unprecedented amount of £10,035,952. The largest exports in point of value, that ever took place previous to 1850, occurred in the year 1815, when owing to the interruption of intercourse with the United States of America in the two preceding years, the quantities sent to that country were unusually great; the total value amounting to £9,361,426, of which £4,378,195, were sent to the United States. When we consider the quantity of woollen goods exported, does not represent more than two-fifths of the whole produce of the country, some idea of the value of this important branch of manufacture will be obtained; a manufacture giving employment to 350,000 persons.

Like the cotton manufacture, this is one of the branches of trade, the value of which cannot be made apparent by the mere exhibition of specimens of manufacture; it therefore becomes necessary to enter more fully into the statistical and other details of the manufacture, than in the case of some others, which, though more attractive in appearance, contribute a far smaller share to the wealth of the nation.

The manufacture of woollen cloth in England, commenced with, or very soon after the growth of wool, cloths being certainly made here, long before the year 1224. From the time of Edward III, down to the year 1838, wool, and the woollen manufacture, never ceased to be the subject of some import-

either the exportation of wool, or the importation of woollen cloth was prohibited ; or the length, breadth, or weight, of both narrow and broad cloths, regulated by act of parliament—or the export of undyed cloths was prohibited—or an export duty placed on woollen goods exported—or the cupidity of the sovereign as in the case of James I—or the exigencies of the monarch, as in the case of Charles I, granted monopolies, inimical to the interest of the manufacturers ; and it was not until the year 1833, that the last vestige of these restrictions were removed, and the woollen trade left free and unfettered.

As there will be various machines exhibited in actual operation, showing the process of the manufacture of cloth, and other woollen goods, we will confine ourselves to a mere sketch of the processes employed, premising, that previous to the introduction of the cotton-spinning machinery, to be noticed in a subsequent article, all the woollen yarn of the kingdom, was spun by the domestic spinning-wheel ; the woollen manufacture therefore, stands indebted equally with the cotton, to the genius and skill of Hargreaves, Arkwright, and Crompton ; whilst the application of water and steam-power, the introduction of the power-loom, gig-mill, and shearing-frames, together with improved processes of felting, dyeing, and finishing, have enabled us to make a superior article at a far less price than formerly, and to enter into successful competition with the foreign manufacturer, although still to some extent dependant on foreign countries for the wool best adapted to the manufacture of goods of the finer qualities.

In the manufacture of woollen cloth, no small amount of knowledge and skill is necessary : the processes being not only numerous, but requiring much care and attention. When a package of wool is opened, the " sorter" separates it into various sorts or qualities ; it is next scoured in hot alkaline liquor, and washed in running water, and if intended for wool-dyed cloth, it is then dyed. The next process is that of " willying," or " devilling," in order to disentangle the locks of wool, and loosen the fibres, which are then sprinkled with oil, to render the wool softer and more easy to work. The next process is that of " scribbling," by which each individual fibre is effectually separated, and the wool assumes a light flocculent appearance. By the aid of the " carding-machine," the fibres of the scribbled wool, are brought nearly parallel to each other, and rolled up into the form of a pipe, the object being to make the fibres interlace each other more readily and completely, in the after process of fulling. By means of the slubbing-machine, these pipes or cardings are joined together, and spun into continuous lengths ; a pound of wool in general, yielding several thousand yards of " slubbing." It is then spun by the spinning-machine into yarn, and woven by means of the hand or power-loom, into cloth. The cloth when woven, is " milled" or "fulled," with liquid soap* and fuller's earth, by beating in the fulling stocks, by which means, the fibres of the wool are made thoroughly to interlace, and by so doing, the cloth becomes greatly thickened, shortened, and narrowed. A piece of cloth to be sixty inches wide when finished, must be woven nearly one hundred inches wide, and the length adjusted

in the same proportion. The cloth is then dried, and if it is to be piece-dyed, it then undergoes the process of dyeing. The nap of the cloth is next raised, by passing it through "gig-mills," the surfaces of which are covered with teazle heads, and the nap thus raised, is cut or sheared, so as to produce an

* The quantity of soap used in the woollen manufacture in 1849 was 13,054,752 lbs., the excise duty on which, amounting to £45,681 19s., was remitted.

surface, by means of the cutting-machines. There are also a number of minor processes, all calculated to give an improved surface to the cloth; such as boiling it, to impart a certain lustre; burling or picking it, to remove little imperfections; inking any little cotton or linen particles, which may appear in the dyed cloth, arising from the bags in which the wool is

imported; pressing it between hot-iron plates, and smooth mill-board; steaming, and passing the cloth over cylinders, covered either with brushes, or a kind of plush, &c,

The most complete collection of woollen cloths exhibited, is furnished by Messrs. H. J. and D. Nicoll, of Regent-street, and comprises specimens of upwards of 200 varieties of colour, texture and finish. Some of these specimens are characterized by novelty of shade, others by exquisite fineness and suppleness, whilst others, by their brilliancy and gaudiness of colouring, lead us to suppose they must be manufactured merely for show. Such, however, is not the case; cloths of these brilliant colours are designed for the South American and other markets, to which Messrs. Nicoll annually export considerable quantities of woollen cloths.

The success of the woollen cloth manufacture, is not dependent on the mere production of superior cloths, but the taste and skill of the designer, in inventing new modes and forms of dress, are also indispensable. The inelegant, and, in some cases, *outré* appearance of modern costume, have necessarily led to the invention of designs for dress, in which ease and elegance may be combined, and comfort and good taste go hand-in-hand. The splendid collection of costumes, (of which we give a few specimens,) selected from the best authorities, and arranged with scrupulous fidelity and correctness, by Messrs. Nicoll, is intended to illustrate some of the most elegant and useful forms of dress, which have prevailed

from the earliest times, and thus furnish the designer with materials wherewith to improve the costumes of the present day, by the adoption of the tasteful and useful of the past.

It is true, that we too often become deeply rooted in habits and prejudices, even respecting modes and forms of dress, and a dread of singularity, and a dislike of innovation, leads us to cling to old fashions in dress, as well as to old habits of thought. Much of this, however, has arisen from a deficiency of taste and execution in our articles of dress, and is therefore the more readily to be overcome by the display and exhibition of such inventions as those referred to, and which are characterized no less by elegance and good taste, than by comfort and real usefulness. In this

respect, Messrs. Nicoll have attained a well-merited superiority; and whether in the robe of the peer, the gown of the clergyman and barrister, the dress of the court, the ball-room, and the promenade, the riding-habit of the fair equestrian, or the *robe de chambre* of domestic comfort, in each and all, good taste, correctness of design, and real elegance, are uniformly displayed.

The principal seats of the woollen cloth manufacture in this country
are Leeds, Huddersfield, Halifax, and Saddleworth, in Yorkshire; Stroud
and Wootton-under-Edge, in Gloucestershire; and Frome, Bradford, and
Trowbridge, in Wiltshire.

The cloths manufactured in the two last named counties are denomi-
nated West of England cloths, and are superior in quality to those of
Yorkshire. Paisley, Gallashiells, Hawick, and Selkirk, in Scotland,
produce tweeds and tartans. With regard to the other branches of the
woollen manufacture, it will be sufficient merely to mention, Rochdale
and North Wales, as the seats of the flannel manufacture; Dewsbury,
Witney, &c., for blankets; Leeds and Huddersfield, for woollen cloaking;

Halifax and Rochdale, for serges; and Bradford, Halifax, Keighley, Bingley, &c., as the principal seats of the manufacture of an almost endless variety of worsted-stuff goods, composed either entirely of wool and cotton, of wool and silk, of wool, silk, and cotton, or of alpaca and mohair, mixed with cotton or silk, the trade in which, under the name of merinos, de laines, barèges, camlets, cobourgs, orleans, and union cloths, alpaca lustres, and mixtures, has increased so considerably. Bradford, Huddersfield, and Leeds, are the chief seats of the manufacture of woollen yarns.

We notice that the manufacturers of Stroud have carried off the prizes offered by Messrs. Bull and Wilson, for the finest cloth and doeskin manufactured in England, the gold medal having been awarded to Messrs. J. and D. Apperly, for the former, and to Mr. W. Helme, for the latter.

In 1850, there were imported 72,674,483 lbs. of sheep and lamb's wool, of which 14,054,815 lbs. were re-exported; 1,652,295 lbs. of Alpaca and Llama wool, of which 333,859 lbs. were re-exported. Of woollen manufactures not made up, there were imported to the value of £535,459, of which £115,509 were re-exported. Of articles or manufactures of wool, wholly or in part made up, to the value of £146,583, of which £135,952 were entered for home consumption, and £11,584 export d. Of sheep and lamb's wool, of British and Irish produce, there were ex orted, in 1850, 12,000,459 lbs., of the declared value of £623,964. Of woollen manufactures, entered by the piece, 2,778,724 pieces, of the value o. £5,383,062 : ditto, entered by the yard, 63,731,053 yards, of the value of £2,876,848. Of all other descriptions (except stockings, elsewhere mentioned), to the value of £259,467. Of woollen yarn, 123,151 cwts., of the value of £1,451,098.

Total value of exports of woollen goods and yarn in 1850, was £10,025,952, and £8,482,496 in 1849. The total value of the woollen trade of this country, is estimated at £25,000,000 per annum.

The number of woollen factories in this country is 1,497, containing 1,595,278 spindles, and 9,439 power-looms, the moving power of the machinery being—steam, representing 13,455 horse-power, and water, 8,689 horse-power, and the number of persons employed, 74,443. The number of worsted factories is 501, containing 875,830 spindles, and 32,617 power-looms, worked by steam of 9,890, and water 1,625 horse-power, and employing 79,737 persons. If to these we add the great body of hand-loom weavers and persons employed in making and repairing machinery, a total of more than 350,000 will be obtained.

The United States of America, the Hanseatic Towns, British North America, Australia, Holland, Belgium, Portugal, Turkey, Continental India, China, and the South American States, are the countries to which we export the largest quantities of our woollen manufactures. Australia, the Hanseatic Towns, British India, the British possessions in South Africa, and the Russian ports within the Black Seas, and Buenos Ayres, supply us with a large porportion of the foreign sheep and lamb's wool used in our manufactures; whilst Peru and Chili furnish us with the produce of the alpaca and Llama tribe.

Our chief supplies of foreign wool were at one period derived from Spain, and subsequently from Germany, but the rapid development of our colonial possessions in Australia and South Africa, has led to our now receiving by far our chief supply of imported wool from those quarters, as the following account of the importation of 1849 will clearly show.

The wool imported from our colonies in Australia, which, in 1815, amounted to only 73,171 lbs., is now equal to upwards of 35,879,971 lbs.; while the imports from Spain, which in 1815 were fully 6,627,934 lbs., have now dwindled down to 107,559 lbs. In the same period from the northern towns of Germany, the imports have reached as high as 31,766,194 lbs., but do not now exceed 12,750,071 lbs. From other countries of Europe, the quantity received in 1849 was below the average of the last ten years. The produce of the Cape of Good Hope has increased from 23,363 lbs. to 5,377,405 lbs.; that of the British possessions in India from 3,721 lbs., in 1834, to 4,182,853 lbs. in 1849; and fiom South America the importations in the same period have shown a large increase. The total importation of wool into Great Britian in 1849 was 73,768,647 lbs., of which, as has been previously shown, 41,257,466 lbs. is the produce of our colonies in Australia and the Cape of Good Hope, and of the remainder about 22,653,631 is the produce of countries in which our manufactured goods find a ready market in exchange, while a comparatively insignificant portion is drawn from those countries in which heavy duties or other restrictions are placed upon goods of British production. The value of the colonial wool imported exceeds three millions sterling, which amount is expended in payment for British goods.

In 1850, there were imported into France 50,455,104 lbs. of sheep and lambswool, and 2,284 cwts. of woollen goods exported. The value of the woollen goods exported in 1849, was £5,200,000.

Sedan, Elbeuf, and Louviers, are the principal seats of the woollen cloth manufacture in France; whilst Castres mostly furnishes merinoes and fancy goods. The estimated value of the woollen cloths manufactured in France is 300,000,000 francs (£12,000,000) per annum.

The mousseline de laines, and goods of wool mixed with cotton or silk, are made principally at Roubaix, Paris, Rheims, and Amiens; and the annual production is estimated at 180,000,000 francs (£7,200,000.) Large quantities of woollen cloths are manufactured at Verviers, in Belgium; and at Aix le Chapelle, and the district of the Lower Rhine, in Prussia.

SILK MANUFACTURE.

Fabrication de Soie. Seiden Manufactur.

———

THE silk manufacture of England is by more than two centuries the junior of the woollen manufacture, having been introduced in the 15th century. Like its elder sister, the silk trade has been the subject of legislative interference and protection, which has opened the door for fraud and smuggling to an immense amount, and been detrimental to the interests of the home trade. The abolition of the prohibition system in 1826, and the liberal measures subsequently adopted, have materially improved, instead of injuring the trade; for whilst in 1821-2-3, when the restrictive system was in full rigour, the raw and thrown silk imported did not exceed 2,329,000 lbs., the importation of 1850 reached 5,427,543 lbs., nearly 125 per cent. increase upon the quantity entered during the existence of the monopoly.

Whilst the raw material in the cotton and woollen manufactures comes to us in the form of short fibres, requiring to be spun into a continuous thread, in the silk manufacture, the spinning process is performed by the silk worm itself, who presents the material in a continuous form. The worm having been stifled in the cocoon or egg-shaped envelope it has formed, the floss silk forming the external soft envelope is first removed, and afterwards brought to a manufactured state, by the process of silk spinning, while the cocoon itself passes into the hands of the silk throwster, who winds off the thread of several cocoons together, passing the combined thread round a hollow frame or reel; the original silk filament as elaborated by the insect being so fine, as to require nearly 500 miles of length to weigh one pound.

The hanks of silk thus produced from the cocoons by the silk reelers of Italy, France, Bengal, China, and other countries, form the commodity which arrives in England under the name of *raw silk*. That which is imported under the name of *thrown* silk, is the article after having been worked in the silk mills of foreign countries. The quantity of raw silk imported into England in 1850, was 4,958,017 lbs., and of thrown silk 469,526 lbs., and as it takes 250 cocoons on the average to weigh one pound, the average quantity of silk imported as above, may be considered as the produce of 1,356,885,750 worms.

The processes which the raw silk undergoes in its passage through the silk mill, depend on the purposes to which the silk is to be applied. The principal operations are those of winding, cleaning, doubling, and twisting or throwing. The process of winding the silk, is accomplished by placing the skeins or hanks of raw silk on swifts, whence the silk is wound on bobbins four or five inches in length. The cleaning process comes next, by which the removal of all impurities or irregularities is effected, and the diameter of the thread rendered equal; it consists merely in passing the silken thread through a cleft in a piece of steel, so adjusted in size, as to allow the thread in its proper state of thickness to pass freely through, but to detain and remove all asperities, roughnesses, and irregularities of surface. The silk, called in this state *dumb singles,* is now ready for the weaving of gauze and other thin fabrics. In order to prepare the silk thread for the weaving of ribbons and common silks, it must go through the additional process of twisting or throwing, which is accomplished by passing the thread from a horizontal revolving bobbin, fixed on spindles, through a loop or eye attached to one end, and fastened to a stationary vertical bobbin; motion being given to the apparatus, the thread becomes wound on the vertical bobbin, by the rotation of the little loop apparatus, called the "flyer," round this bobbin, and a twist is at the same time imparted to the thread. The hardness or closeness of the twist can be regulated by the silk throwster at pleasure, by varying the velocities of the two moving parts. This silk is called *thrown singles.* The silk thread used for the weft or cross threads of Gros de Naples, velvets, flowered silks, and the best varieties of silk goods is called *tram silk.* In addition to the previous operations, it goes through the process of doubling, or combining two or more threads into one, to increase the strength or thickness.

Another kind called *organzine,* besides being wound, cleaned, and doubled, is twisted or thrown twice, the first twist being like the yarns which form a strand, and the second like the strands which form a rope; this forms a hard and compact thread, and is used as the warp or long threads, for the same kind of goods as those which have tram in the weft. Sewing silk, is formed of compound threads of silk, wound, cleaned, doubled, and thrown with a special reference to its ultimate use. The dyeing or bleaching of the silk is generally effected immediately, or soon after the twisting is finished, having previously been passed through the scouring process, which consists of boiling the thread three or four hours in strong soap* and water, by which the gummy matter is dissolved, and the silk rendered soft and glossy. Derby has continued to be the principal seat of the silk-throwing trade, ever since its introduction into this country from Italy. The average weekly quantity of raw silk thrown in Derby, is

---

* The quantity of soap used in the silk manufacture in 1849, was 1,601,471 lbs., the excise duty on which, amounting to £14,991 15s., was remitted.

11,500 lbs. The silk is now ready for the weaver, and according to its various qualities is sent to those places where the different kinds of manufactured silk goods are prepared.

The weaving of silk goods is performed in the same way as that of cotton and woollen fabrics. In Spitalfields, the weavers work in their own houses, and employ the hand-loom for their plain goods, and the Jacquard loom for fancy goods. In Manchester, Derby, and other places, the power-loom has been successfully applied to the weaving of silk goods. Although the chief part of the ribbons produced at Coventry and the surrounding district is still a domestic manufacture, yet the factory system and the power-loom are gradually being introduced.

As the Jacquard loom will be shewn in operation at the Exhibition, we need only call the attention of the visitor to the beauty of the silk and other fabrics obtained by its use. By means of an instrument called a pantograph, exquisite embroidery is produced in plain silk goods after weaving.

It need scarcely be remarked that plain silk, like other woven fabrics, consist of threads crossing each other at right angles; the "long threads" being technically called the *warp*, and the cross threads the *shoot* or *weft*. On inspecting either silk or cotton velvet, it will at once be evident, that it possesses some additional feature in its construction. Although the back of the velvet shows the warp and shoot, with more or less distinctness, the face presents the appearance of a short shag or "pile," as it is termed, forming the characteristic of this class of goods. We have no space to go into the minutiæ of the process, but we may just say, that this "pile" is occasioned by the insertion of short pieces of silk-thread, doubled under the shoot, forming a series of loops, standing up from the surface of the silk, and by subsequently cutting these loops with a sharp instrument, called a *trevat*, the pile is produced. It is considered to amount to a very good day's work, when as much as one yard of plain velvet has been woven.

We must not omit to mention, how the resources of modern manufacturing skill, have been successfully brought to bear in working up the floss silk forming the outer covering of the cocoon, and the waste produced in the several operations of spinning and throwing we have before mentioned. This formerly useless material, is now spun into yarn at Manchester, for cheap shawls, handkerchiefs, &c., opening up an entirely new branch of manufacture.

In 1850, there were imported of silk manufactures of Europe, 309,214 lbs. weight of silk or satin broadstuffs, of which 177,501 lbs. were entered for home consumption, and 139,368 lbs. were exported; 280,288 lbs. of silk or satin ribbons imported, of which 167,956 lbs. were entered for home consumption, and 112,102 exported; 6,848 lbs. of gauze or crape broadstuffs imported, of which 5,349 lbs. were retained for home consumption, and 1,731 exported; 44,531 lbs. of gauze or crape ribbons imported, of which 42,796 lbs. were retained for home consumption, and 79 exported; of gauze mixed with silk, satin, or any other materials, in less proportion than one-half of the fabric, viz:— Broadstuffs, 4 lbs.; Ribbons, 2,511, of which 2,498 were retained for home use, and 21 exported; of velvet broadstuffs, 27,674 lbs. were imported, of which 26,397 were retained for home consumption, and 1,841 exported; of ribbons of velvet, or silk embossed with velvet, 16,675 lbs., of which 16,043 were entered for home consumption, and 1,063 exported; of plush for making hats, 188,909, of which 185,029 were retained for home use, and 3,880 exported; of silk manufactures of India, 715,739 pieces of bandannas and other silk handkerchiefs were imported, of which 221,417 were entered for home consumption, and 410,473 exported.

Of British and Irish silk manufactures, there were exported in 1850, of silk only,—Stuffs, handkerchiefs, and ribbons, 424,073 lbs., of the declared value of £487,941; of all other descriptions (except stockings mentioned elsewhere), to the value of £186,288. Of silk, mixed with other materials,— stuffs, handkerchiefs, and ribbons, 760,417 lbs., of the value of £328,966. Of all other descriptions (except stockings), to the value of £23,867. The total value of silk goods, twist, and yarn exported, was £1,265,451.

The number of silk factories in this country is 277, containing 1,225,560 spindles, and 6,092 power-looms, the moving power being—steam, represented by 2,858 horse-power, and water, by 853 horse-power. The number of persons employed in these factories is 42,544, and if to these we add the persons employed in the various branches of domestic silk manufacture, the total number will amount to at least 70,000.

We are indebted to Italy, China, the East Indies, Turkey, and France, for supplies of raw silk. The principal markets for our manufactured silks are our North American colonies, the West India Islands, and the United States of America.

The principal seats of the silk trade in England, are London (Spitalfields), Manchester, Macclesfield, Congleton, Leek, &c., for plain and fancy silks, velvets, &c.; Paisley, Norwich, &c., for gauzes and crapes; Derby, for silk-yarn; and Coventry and district, for ribbons.

Lyons, Nismes, Avignon, and Paris, are the chief seats of the silk manufacture in France, the neighbourhoods of St. Etienne and St. Chamond supplying the market with ribbons. French silks and ribbons of the value of £791,711 were imported into England in 1849.

In 1850 France imported 4,881,408 lbs. of raw silk, in addition to her home produce, and exported 4,095,840 lbs. of manufactured silks. The value of manufactured silks exported in 1849 was £7,240,000; of raw silk £160,000; and of dyed silk £120,000.

The total value of the silk manufactured in France, is at present estimated at 300,000,000 francs, or about £12,000,000, one-third of which consists of the value of the material used, the remaing two-thirds of value, being added for labour and profit. The result of the manufacture in both countries is placed in very striking contrast, by the fact, that whilst two-thirds of the silk goods made in France are exported, leaving, consequently, for the use of her 36,000,000 millions of inhabitants, silk fabrics far below the value of £4,000,000 sterling, the exports of English made silk goods, does not amount to one-tenth of the quantity that passes through our looms, and is more than replaced by the goods of foreign manufacture imported for use; so that taking into the calculation the difference in the number of the people, and the greater cost of production, the consumption of silk goods is more than five times as great in the United Kingdom, as it is in France. Not the least surprising of the effects which have followed the total alteration of our system in regard to the silk manufacture is, that of our now exporting silk goods to France to a considerable amount. In 1849, the value of silk goods exported to France, amounted to £159,973, being more than three-eighths of the whole value exported to the Continent. The superiority of the French weaver which existed for so many years, is now almost entirely removed, and as regards the texture of silk fabrics, the produce of the English loom is fully equal to the silk goods of our neighbours. If we are behind them in any respect, it is in the invention of patterns, and the combination of colours; but these deficiencies are being fast remedied; we can get the raw material as cheap as they can, taking one quality with another; we have better machinery; capital in greater abundance; while our manufacturing skill, and commercial enterprize, enables us to set all other nations at defiance, as regards the great productions of manufacturing industry.

It may not be uninteresting to mention here the results obtained by M. Nourrigat, a cultivator of silk-worms at Lunel, in the department of Herault, in France, during the last year. From 24 ozs. of eggs, he obtained silk-worms sufficient to produce upwards of 32 cwts. of cocoons, the worms requiring for their food 640 cwts. of mulberry leaves, or 100 leaves for every 5 of cocoons. The cocoons were sold for £306 10s.; the expenses were £108 5s., and the net profit £198 10s.

The successful results of the experiments of Mr. Felkin, the present Mayor of Nottingham, in the rearing of silk-worms, and the quality of the silk obtained by him, leaves no doubt of the possibility, where labour can be obtained at a cheap rate, of obtaining a large supply of raw silk in our own country.

COTTON MANUFACTURE.

Fabrication de Coton.   *Baumwollen Manufactur.*

As it will be impossible fully to illustrate this most important branch of manufacture so as to give the visitor any correct idea of its extent and value, we propose to furnish a few particulars relative to the past and present condition of the cotton manufacture of our own country, with remarks on the extent of this manufacture in some other countries.

Fortunately for the cotton manufacture of this country, it has never been like the woollen and silk manufactures—the object of legislative protection; the cotton manufacturers have, therefore, been obliged to put forth all their powers—to avail themselves of every resource of science and of art—and the consequence has been, that they have raised the British cotton manufacture from a subordinate place, to that of the first rank in the manufactures of the world.

Up to the year 1760, the machines used in the cotton manufacture in England, were nearly as simple as those of India, though the loom was more perfectly and strongly constructed, and cards for combing the cotton had been adopted from the woollen manufacture. But the great impediment to the progress of the cotton manufacture, was the impossibility of obtaining an adequate supply of yarn; since every thread used in the manufacture of cotton, (as well as wool, worsted, and flax,) throughout the world, was spun singly by the fingers of the spinner, with the aid of that classical instrument, the domestic spinning-wheel. The one-thread wheel, though turning from morning to night, in thousands of cottages, could not keep pace either with the weaver's shuttle or the demand of the merchant. Genius stepped in to remove the difficulty, and gave wings to a manufacture, which had been creeping on the earth. In 1767, an eight-handed spinster sprung from the genius of Hargreaves; and the *jenny*, with still increasing powers, made its way into common use, in spite of all opposition. In 1738, a mechanical contrivance was invented by John Wyatt, of Birmingham patented in the name of Lewis Paul, by which 20, 50, 100, or even 1,000 threads could be spun at once by a single pair of hands. The invention, however, slumbered for nearly thirty years, when it was either re-discovered by Arkwright, or what is more probable, its principles came accidentally to his knowledge. The keen sagacity of Arkwright soon appreciated its value, and his perseverance, good fortune, and talent, enabled him by its means to enrich himself and his country. Weavers could now obtain an unlimited supply of yarn at a reasonable price; manufacturers could use warps of cotton, which were much cheaper than the linen warps formerly employed; cotton fabrics could be sold cheaper; and the demand for them steadily increased. The factory system now commenced in England, and large mills were erected for the manufacture of cotton goods. Five years later, the happy thought of combining these two inventions to produce a third, more efficient than either, struck the mind of Crompton, who, by a perfectly original contrivance, effected the union. From 20 spindles this machine was brought, by more finished mechanism, to admit of 100 spindles, and thus to exercise a five-fold power. Before the discovery of the *mule-jenny*, or *mule* of Crompton, it was supposed impossible to spin 80 hanks to the pound, but now as many as 520 hanks to the pound have been spun, each hank measuring 840 yards, and forming together a thread of upwards of 248 miles in length. The application, first of water-power by Kelly, and subsequently of steam-power, by Watt, as a substitute for the toilsome method of turning the machine by hand, gave a further impetus to the development of the cotton manufacture; and the invention of the power-loom by Cartwright, and the successive improvements effected by Roberts and others, in the construction both of the mule and the power loom, have produced effects, whose influence have been most marvellous in augmenting the wealth and population of the country.

The cotton is brought to the mill in bags, just as it is received from Egypt, India, or America, and is then stowed in warehouses, being arranged according to the countries from which it may have come. It is first passed through the *willow*, which, by its revolving spikes, tears open the cotton, and by the blast of a powerful fan, frees it from most of its dirt and seeds. It is then taken to the scutching machine, in which it is subjected to be beaten by metallic blades, revolving in an axis at the speed of from 4,000 to 7,000 revolutions in a minute, so that the fibres are opened, and the seeds and dirt fall down through a frame of wire-work. It is then taken to the spreading, or lapping machine, in order to be opened, cleaned, and evenly spread. By the carding engine the fibres are combed out, and laid parallel to each other, and the fleece is compressed into a sliver.

The sliver is repeatedly drawn and doubled in the drawing-frame, in order to straighten the fibres more perfectly, and to equalise the grist. The roving machine, by means of rollers and spindles, produces a coarse and loose thread, which the mule or throstle spins into yarn. To make the warp, the twist is transferred from cops to bobbins by the winding machine, and from the bobbins at the warping mill to a cylindrical beam; this beam being taken to the dressing-machine, the warp is sized, dressed, and wound upon the weaving-beam. The latter is then placed in the hand, or the power loom, by which machine, the shuttle being provided with cops of weft, the cloth is woven.

For sizing the warp, a paste made of flour and water is employed, and a calculation which has been made as to the quantity of flour thus annually consumed shows, that 250,000 power looms, (one-half employed on heavy, and the other half on light goods,) and 250,000 hand looms, together require 71,500,000 lbs. of flour per annum, which, at 35s. the sack of 280 lbs. is equal to £446,874. If to this we add one-third more for flour used in the process of bleaching, &c., we obtain the enormous amount of £595,832 annually required to be spent in this single department of the cotton manufacture.

THE ABOVE ENGRAVING REPRESENTS

RYE'S REGISTERED TAKING-UP ROLLER,

For power looms. The object of the above roller is, to supersede those made of wood, and covered with ground glass or emery. The frequent complaints of the timber giving way, and the covering coming off, rendered it necessary to invent something that would stand all temperatures without flinching. The above roller is made of cast iron, chased from the centre right and left, and afterwards fluted. It thus holds the cloth without slipping, and, at the same time, tends to stretch it wider; it also answers well when wet weft is used, the roller being varnished to prevent rust. Upwards of a thousand of these improved rollers are now in use. They are manufactured by Messrs. Sevill and Woolstenhulme, machine-makers, Oldham-street, Manchester, who are well known for their manufacture of carding engines, power looms, patent sizing and warping machinery, steam engines, &c., of very superior construction.

In a cotton mill containing 50,000 spindles, 700 people are sufficient to attend to the various operations, and by the assistance of the steam engine, are enabled to spin as much thread as 200,000 persons could do without machinery, or one person can do as much as 266. It would require 75,000,000 persons to accomplish by hand, the cotton spinning at present effected by machinery. Each spindle in a mill will produce between 2½ and 3 hanks, (of 840 yards each,) which is upwards of 1½ mile of thread in 12 hours; so that the 50,000 spindles in one mill alone, will produce 62,500 miles of thread every day of 12 hours, which is more than a sufficient length to go 2½ times round the globe. In 1760, there were about 40,000 persons employed in the cotton manufacture.

The superiority of the cotton manufacture of India, is due to a physical organization in the natives, admirably suited to the processes of spinning and weaving; to the possession of the raw material in the greatest abundance; to the possession also of the most brilliant dyes for staining and printing the cloth; to a climate which renders the colours lively and durable; and to the hereditary practice by particular castes, classes, and families, both of the manual operations and chemical processes required in the manufacture. It is to these causes, with very little aid from science, and in an almost barbarous state of the mechanical arts, that India owes her long supremacy in the manufacture of cotton. This effeminate people are remarkable for the fine sense of touch possessed by them, which is altogether unrivalled; the flexibility of the fingers is equally remarkable. The women spin the thread destined for the cloth, and then deliver it to the men, who have fingers to model it as exquisitely as these have prepared it. The rigid clumsy fingers of an European, would scarcely be able to make a piece of canvas, with the instruments which an Indian employs in making a piece of cambric muslin.

Bengal is celebrated for the production of the finest muslins; the Corromandel Coast for the best chintzes and calicos; and Surat for strong and inferior goods of every kind. Table-cloths of superior quality are made at Patna. The *basins*, or *bassinets*, come from the Northern Circars; Condavar furnishes the beautiful handkerchiefs of Masoulipatam, the fine colours of which are partly obtained from a plant, called *chage*, which grows on the banks of the Krishna, and on the coast of the Bay of Bengal. The chintzes and ginghams are chiefly made at Masoulipatam, Madras, St. Thomé, and Paliameotta. The long-cloths and fine pullicals are produced in the Presidency of Madras; the coarse piece goods, as well as common muslins and chintzes, are extensively manufactured in the district of which Surat is the port.

The British navigator now brings the cotton of India from a distance of several thousand miles, manufactures it, carries back the manufactured article to India, and, in spite of the loss of time, and enormous expense incurred by this voyage, the cotton manufactured by the machinery of England becomes less costly, than the cotton of India spun and woven by the hand near the field that produced it, and sold at the nearest market,—so great is the power of the progress of machinery.

The natural and physical advantages of England for manufacturing industry, are, probably, superior to those of any other country on the globe. The districts where those advantages are found in the most favourable combination, are the southern part of Lancashire, and the south-western part of Yorkshire,—the former of which has become the principal seat of the cotton manufacture. In the counties of Cheshire, Derbyshire, and Nottinghamshire; and in Renfrewshire and Lanarkshire, in Scotland; all of which districts are likewise seats of this branch of industry, advantages of a similar nature are found; though not in such close concentration as in Lancashire. These advantages are—abundance of water-power; good supply of coal for fuel; and iron for machinery, with abundance of pure water for dyeing and bleaching operations. Manchester, Glasgow, Carlisle, Paisley, Preston, and Lancashire generally, are the principal places in which this important manufacture is located.

The following account of the importations and exportations connected with the cotton manufacture in the year 1850, is taken from official sources :—*Imports.*—Raw cotton, 5,934,798 cwts. (against 6,745,259 cwts. in 1849). Cotton yarn, 905,966 lbs., of the declared value of £97,561. Cotton manufactures not made up,—East India piece goods, 186,010 pieces of the value of £68,938. Other articles to the value of £297,176. Cotton manufactures wholly or in part made up to the value of £44,815. *Exports.*—Foreign and Colonial manufacture—Cotton manufactures not made up,—East India piece goods, 145,895 pieces of the value of £58,493. Other articles to the value of £98,605. Of cotton manufactures wholly or in part made up, to the value of £23,667. Cotton yarn, 777,957 lbs., to the value of £81,014. British cotton manufactures, (exclusive of lace, patent net, sewing thread, and stockings, an account of which will appear in their proper place,) 1,358,238,887 yards, to the value of £20,528,150. Other descriptions, to the value of £236,058. Cotton yarn, 131,438,188 lbs., valued at £6,360,948.

The quantity of raw cotton consumed in the cotton manufacture of Great Britain in the year 1850, was 584,200,000 lbs., or nearly 900 tons per diem.

The total number of cotton factories in this country is 1,932; containing 20,977,017 spindles, and 249,627 power-looms. The moving power in these factories is supplied by—steam, representing 71,005 horse-power, and water, 11,550 horse-power, the total number of persons employed in these factories amounting to 330,924. If to these we add the persons not employed in factories, such as hand-loom weavers, calico printers and dyers, makers and repairers of machinery, &c., a total of 790,000 would be obtained.

The total value of the cotton goods and yarn exported, in 1850, was £28,252,878; in 1849, £26,775,135. The capital employed in the cotton manufacture of Great Britain is not less than £45,000,000.

We receive our supply of raw cotton from the United States of America, the East Indies, Brazil, and Egypt, and export our manufactured produce chiefly to the East Indies, Brazil, and Turkey; and, in a less degree, to almost every part of the habitable globe.

Twenty-five years ago America did not possess a single cotton factory, whilst in 1849, 517,000 cwts. of cotton were that year consumed by the American manufacturers. The cotton manufacture is confined to six States —Maine, New Hampshire, Vermont, Massachusetts, Rhode Island, and Connecticut. The quantity of raw cotton consumed in 1850 was about 188,000,000 lbs. The number of spindles may be estimated at 6,000,000.

The principal seat of the cotton manufacture in France, is Rouen, which may be termed the French "Manchester." There are at Rouen and its vicinity, 292 factories, with 1,890,000 spindles. Next comes Mulhouse and its district; then Lille, St. Quentin, and Amiens. The total number of spindles in the cotton factories of France, is about 4,300,000. The quantity of raw cotton consumed in the factories of France, in 1850, was about 142,000,000 lbs. The capital engaged in the manufacture may be estimated at £10,000,000; and the number of persons employed at 260,000.

The quantity of raw cotton imported into France, in 1850, was 1,168,806 cwts. (against 1,283,390 cwts. in 1849.) The value of the cotton goods exported from France, in 1849, was £5,920,000.

The quantity of raw cotton consumed in 1850 by other manufacturing countries, may be estimated as follows:—Russia, Germany, Holland, and Belgium, 133,000,000 lbs., employing upwards of 4,000,000 spindles; Spain, 29,000,000 lbs., with 900,000 spindles; the Mediterranean, 11,000,000 lbs., with 350,000 spindles; and the countries bordering on the Adriatic, 45,000,000 lbs., employing about 1,400,000 spindles.

The first calico-printing concern established in England, was founded by a Frenchman, a short time prior to the year, 1700. For a number of years the fabric was printed with a wooden block, on which the figures were cut in relief,—a mode of printing still adopted for certain kinds of goods. Attempts were made to substitute long and short wooden rollers, but little appears to have been achieved by this method. In 1785, the cylinder machine was introduced and successfully applied. In this machine we see the element of that enormous amount of production, that is going on at the present day, by which miles of calico are printed with incredible rapidity and accuracy, for (apart from the fact, that very much of the work executed by cylinders, could not be done by blocks *with any amount of labour*); as much work can be executed by a cylinder machine in a few minutes, under the superintendance of *one* man, as could be done by a *hundred* men and girls by the hand-block in a whole day. Dalton's new cylinder machine, for printing *on both sides of the calico at the same time*, will be an object of great interest in the Exhibition.

In 1833, the duty of 5d. per yard on printed calicoes was repealed, it having been satisfactorily shown that of the £200,000 derived from this import, not less than £100,000 went to pay the cost of collection.

We close this rough sketch of the cotton manufacture with a few remarks on the sewing cotton trade of Leicester.

Upwards of 500 hands are employed in winding cotton, and in manufacturing reels. The winding department is attended to by young women, one of whom can attend to the winding of from 5,000 to 6,000 reels per week, or about 312,000 per annum, each reel containing 100 yards. The number of yards of cotton put on the reels varies from 50 to 2,000 yards. In the larger houses the machinery for winding is worked by steam; (about 9,000 revolutions being made per minute;) in houses in a smaller way of business, the machinery is turned by the hand. Sewing cotton is not spun in Leicester, but is brought in bundles weighing 10 lbs. each, varying in price from 10s. to £9; and varying in length from 40,000 to 200,000 yards. Most of the winders manufacture their own reels. A hand-turner is capable of turning off about gross per week of reels, containing 100 yards of cotton; of larger reels a less number in proportion. One of the larger houses has now superseded the hand-turning by machinery, by the help of which a boy can turn off 200 gross per week, at the cost of a halfpenny per gross, while a man's wages for hand-turning is about sixpence per gross.

LINEN MANUFACTURE.

Fabrication de Lin.   Leinwand Manufactur.

Up to an early period in the present century, all the linen yarns were produced by hand-spinning, which was carried on as in the case of the cotton and woollen trades, by women in their cottages throughout the country. These were brought by them to the nearest town on market days, where they were purchased by the weavers; or in many cases, the female members of a family spun the yarn, which was woven by the men. For so long a period had this method been pursued, that the spinning-wheel became emblematic of manufactures in general, and the term *spinster* remains the legal appellation of our unmarried females to the present day. The use of the spinning-wheel was not entirely confined to the humbler classes of society, but often found its way into higher circles. In 1793, the first machinery for spinning flax was erected in Great Britain. In 1841, there were in Ireland 41 mills, with 260,000 spindles in operation; and there are now, in 1851, about 75 mills, with 400,000 spindles, actively employed.

The flax is brought from the flax farmers, in the form of small bundles, called "heads," measuring about two feet in length, and weighing a few pounds each. The dust and dirt are first removed by preparatory processes, and the heads of the flax are next "scutched" out at the ends, by means of a machine, which subjects the ends of the fibres to a rude sort of combing or beating. They are then cut or broken into two pieces, so as to divide each fibre into three portions, which differ in quality, the middle one being the best. The next process is that of "heckling," the object of which is, to remove every particle of extraneous matter, and to arrange the whole of the filaments in distinct, even, and parallel layers.

These several processes can only be considered as the first stage of manufacture, and the result of them is to reduce, on the average, full one-half of the original fibre to a low material, called *tow*, which does not exceed one-half of the original value, whereby the other and better half, or *line*, is greatly enhanced in price, having to sustain not only the loss of difference in value on the tow, but also the value of the unnecessary waste made in the processes, and the cost of these processes. This is one great cause why linen goods cost so much more than cotton goods, although the raw material of flax is of less value than cotton.

The heckled flax having been sorted, it next undergoes the drawing process, which is somewhat analogous to the formation of a continuous band or sliver, as mentioned under the woollen manufacture; the tow also undergoes a process of being drawn into slivers. These slivers, whether of *line* or of *tow*, are next transformed to the state of a soft, small, cylindrical cord, by means of the roving frame, in which the sliver is drawn out or elongated, and it has, at the same time, a slight twist imparted to it, to enable it to cohere, and to bear the subsequent operations of the spinning machines.

The flax or tow is next spun, for which purpose it is previously immersed in warm water, experience having shown that a finer and smoother yarn could thus be obtained, If intended for weaving, the spun yarn is then reeled into hanks; but if the yarn is to be made into thread, it is carried to other machines, by means of which two yarn threads are twisted together, and thus is formed the hard and firm thread used in needlework and lace making.

The flax yarn thus produced is then woven into any kind of linen or flaxen fabric, and, according to the degree of fineness or coarseness of the yarn, will be that of the goods produced.

The principal seats of the linen manufacture are—Belfast, Dundee, Forfar, Kirkaldy, &c., for plain linens, Irish linens, and shirtings; Lisburn and Belfast, for damasks; Lurgan, for cambric and lawn; Armagh and Dunfermline, for light linens; Ballymena, for heavy linens; Carlisle, &c., for thread; Barnsley, for duck, check, diaper, and union; Dundee, for canvas. The largest quantities of yarn are spun at Leeds, Belfast, Dundee, and Huddersfield.

Some idea of the progressive improvements which have been made in the fine linen manufacture, may be obtained from the fact, that whilst in 1828, for every 1000 pieces of French cambric imported, there were but 100 pieces of Irish cambric made; in 1845 15,000 of the latter were sold for each 1000 of the former. Fine hand-spun yarn, of the value of £40,000 to £50,000, is annually imported from Westphalia, for the manufacture of cambric; the machine-spun linen yarn not being fine enough for the purpose.

In 1850, there were imported 1,321,578 cwts. of flax and tow, or codilla of hemp and flax. Of linen manufactures,—lawns, not French, to the value of £2,049, of which £848 worth were entered for home consumption. Cambrics and French lawns, 30,384 pieces, of which 28,256 were entered for home consumption. Damask and damask diaper, 17,882 square yards, of which 16,653 square yards were entered for home consumption. Plain linen and diaper, and manufactures unenumerated, not made up, of the value of £30,065; sails and articles wholly, or in part made up, of the value of £8,534, of which £7,212 worth were entered for home consumption. Plain linen and diaper, of foreign manufacture, was exported to the value of £9,483. Of British and Irish manufactured linens, there were exported, in 1850, 122,897,457 yards, of the declared value of £3,594,944, (exclusive of lace of thread, referred to under lace). Thread for sewing, 3,361,922 lbs., of the declared value of £330,328; linen of all other descriptions, to the value of £17,722, and of linen yarn, 18,559,318 lb, of the value of £887,295. Of undressed hemp, 1,048,685 cwts. were imported. The total value of the exports in 1850, £4,845,030.

There 393 flax factories in this country, containing 965,031 spindles, and 1,141 power-looms, worked by steam of 10,905 horse-power, and water of 3,397 horse-power. The number of persons employed is 68,434; but if we add to this the number employed in hand-loom weaving and various domestic branches of the manufacture, the total number employed in this manufacture will be found to be not far short of 300,000.

In the northern departments of France there are 58 flax-spinning mills, containing 129,000 spindles, and the annual value of their production is estimated at £1,200,000.

We import flax, &c., chiefly from Russia, Holland, Egypt, and Belgium; and export our linen manufactures principally to the United States of America, British West Indies, and St. Thomas, Brasil, Mexico, and the Hanseatic Towns.

The Irish flax is considered the best for the majority of purposes; in 1849, there were 60,073 acres of land in Ireland, under flax cultivation.

We must not here omit to notice the improvements which have recently been patented by Mr. Robert Plummer, of Newcastle, in the machinery and processes employed in the manufacture of flax and other fibrous materials. From a consideration of the destruction of so large a portion of this valuable fibre in the processes employed in the earliest stage of its manufacture, Mr. Plummer was convinced, that not only might improvements be made in the machines employed, but that still greater advantages would accrue from improved methods of treating the fibre when submitted to the action of those machines, treating in fact, the fibre with more tenderness, and thus saving considerable loss, and at the same time giving greater facility for avoiding cutting, and for dealing with flax in the original length and integrity of its fibre.

As one step towards obtaining these advantageous and desirable results, Mr. Plummer uses brushes made of elastic materials, as of split whalebone, for instance, in place of the rigid heckles at present employed. The effects of this substitution of brushes in the preparation of line are to produce greater cleanliness both in the line and in the tow; the shive, gum and dirt, being fully loosened and precipitated to the ground; to give a considerably greater yield of line from paralizing the fibres by the brushes, before they are struck by the rigid heckle pins; to produce a finer fibre from a less amount of the dressing; to subdue greatly the root and top ends of the flax; and, as a consequence of these, to save materially in the heckles of the machines, and in the filleting of the cards; to promote in all the future processes greater purity of sliver and evenness of work, with less waste; and ultimately to produce a cleaner, leveller, and brighter yarn. It has been found in practice, that the improvement in the yield of *line*, is from 3 to 9 pounds per cwt., both in long and cut flax, the line being at the same time cleaner and better dressed.

Mr. Plummer has also introduced some improvements in the heckling machines themselves, by which also the flax is treated with greater gentleness. One of these heckling machines is a Double Cylinder Machine, the other an Oscillating Double-sheet Machine. The objects sought to be obtained in these machines are, to brush the flax on both sides at one time before heckling, and so that it may pass at once on to the pins without any cross or entangled fibres; to get the flax better spread out in the holder in order to expose it more regularly to the brushes and pins, by widening and deepening and otherwise improving the holder; to make the brushes and pins work close up to the holder; to make the opposing set of pins intersect and strike the flax so as not to injure the fibre, or the quality of the work; to produce more line and less tow, and to free both from shive and dirt; to cause the machines to deliver the tow they make without the ordinary doffing apparatus ; to secure a larger quantity of work, as regards yield and dressing, than on any single or double machines heretofore in use.   The additional yield obtained from the use of the former of these machines over flat machines, both being furnished with brushes, is from 3 to 4 lbs. per cwt., and in the latter 12 lbs. per cwt.   A pair of the former are capable of dressing 7 cwt. of half-line per diem with six hands, or 5½ cwts. of two-cut line ; they will also dress long flax well ; a pair of the double sheet oscillating machines will dress 11 cwts. of long flax per diem, with six hands.

Mr. Plummer has also introduced some valuable improvements in the construction of the scutching mill, consisting of the substitution of a disc for the arms, and brushes for the blades.   The results obtained by the use of these improved machines are very satisfactory, and fully attest their value.   Mr. Plummer has also made several improvements in the adoption of holders for the flat heckling machines, and the new machines patented by him, in addition to their superior construction, offer the advantage of greater durability.

The brushes have also been applied to hemp most successfully, and the scutching machine opens to rope and twine makers, and to spinners of fine hemp, a cheap and ready mode of cleaning the hemp, whilst the tow thus made, is much preferable to that which falls from the heckle.

Patent Flax Cotton.—We conclude this short sketch of the linen manufacture with a few remarks on the flax cotton, recently patented by M. Claussen, a manufacture which has excited considerable attention of late. The object of M. Claussen's process is, to convert flax into a substance having similar properties to cotton, for manufacturing purposes ; and also, to effect considerable improvements in the bleaching of flax, as well as other textile substances.   This *cottonizing* of the flax is accomplished by steeping the fibre, first, in a dilute acid solution, and subsequently in a solution of carbonate of soda ; by the action of the acid on the soda, a quantity of carbonic acid gas is liberated, the elastic force of which produces a splitting of the fibre of the flax, and converts it into a material which could scarcely be distinguished when it has undergone the bleaching process, from the finest American cotton ; the husk and rigid fibre of the flax assuming the soft texture of the cotton.   M. Claussen states, that the produce obtainable from 100,000 acres of land, (which the company with which he is associated propose to place under flax cultivation in Ireland), will be 96,098 tons of flax ; whereas, by the old method of steeping, only 38,605, and by the most approved method of steeping, 47,410 tons could be obtained.   The manufacture of the flax cotton is being tested on an extensive scale, so that the question of its utility, in a commercial point of view, will speedily be decided.

HOSIERY MANUFACTURE.

Fabrication de Bonneterie et Chaussettes.   Strumpfwaren Manufactur.

AMONGST the various manufactures of Great Britain, of the importance of which, the mere exhibition of their productions does not suffice to give any adequate idea, is that of woollen, cotton, and silk hosiery.   Previous to the time of Elizabeth, stockings were usually knitted of very coarse woollen yarn, or, if desired to be cool and elegant, they were cut out of linen, and sometimes of silk cloth.   The invention of the stocking loom, by the Rev. W. Lee, in 1589, and its subsequent simplification and improvement, led to an entire revolution in the manufacture of hosiery goods.   Whilst, however, water and steam power have been successfully applied to various branches of our manufacturing industry, the stocking trade still remains a domestic employment, for such is the speed of the hands, and the difficulty of "putting in fashion" by power-worked frames, that the superseding of the hand-frame by the latter seems to be very unlikely and remote.

The machines (usually called frames, from which the persons employed at them are usually called framework knitters,) for the manufacture of hosiery, are spread chiefly over 240 parishes in the three midland counties of Nottingham, Leicester, and Derby, and at Tewkesbury, in Gloucestershire, in England; Hawick, Dumfries, Glasgow, and Selkirk, in Scotland; and Dublin and Belfast, in Ireland.   In addition to socks and stockings, large quantities of gloves, and under clothing of various kinds are woven by these frames, and the introduction within the last few years, of a great variety of fancy articles of wool and cotton, such as polkas, neck-ties, ladies' head-dresses, opera caps, &c., &c., has given a great impetus to the hosiery manufacture.   Some idea may be formed of the importance of this branch of trade, when it is stated that the value of the hosiery manufacture of Leicestershire alone, is estimated at upwards of £1,700,000 sterling per annum, and the whole trade throughout the country, at upwards of £3,000,000.   The number of persons employed in the hosiery trade of the kingdom, (independently of spinners included in factory accounts given under cotton, woollen, and silk trades,) is about 45,000.

The number of cotton stockings, of British manufacture, exported in 1850, was 234,163 dozen pairs, of the declared value of £104,434; of silk and mixed stockings, 16,750 dozen pairs, of the value of £23,583; of woollen stockings, 119,873 dozen pairs, of the value of £74,482.

LACE AND BOBBIN-NET MANUFACTURE.

Fabrication de Dentelle, et Dentelle faite à métier.
Spritzen und Bobbinnet Manufactur.

Half a century ago, lace was made principally of *flax* thread, wholly worked by hand, not only in the decorative parts, but in the mesh-work ground itself. The bobbin-net, of modern times, is made of *cotton* thread, the meshes being made wholly by machinery, and the figured device (if any) being effected, sometimes, by the same machine, and at the same time as the ground, and sometimes by a kind of embroidery or tambour-work. The silk net, such as the material of which black veils are sometimes made, is, as its name imports, made of *silk* thread, and is formed by machinery very nearly on the same principle as bobbin-net.

Pillow Lace.—The original manufacture is worked upon a hard stuffed pillow, with silk, flax, or cotton threads, according to a parchment pattern placed upon it, by means of pins, bobbins, and spindles, which are placed and displaced, twisting and interweaving the threads, so as to imitate the pattern designed. This manufacture has long been pursued in almost every town and village in the midland counties, particularly in Buckinghamshire, Bedfordshire, Northamptonshire, besides at Honiton in Devon, and various other places in the West of England. Mr. Biddle, of Oxford-street, London, exhibits some choice specimens of Honiton and pillow lace.

The most celebrated foreign laces are—

1. *Brussels,*—the most valuable. These are two kinds, *Brussels ground,* having a hexagon mesh, formed by platting and twisting four threads of flax, to a perpendicular line of mesh; *Brussels wire ground,* made of silk,—meshes partly straight, and partly arched. The pattern is worked separately, and set on by the needle.

2. *Mechlin,*—a hexagon mesh formed of three flax threads, twisted and platted at the top of the mesh. The pattern is worked in the net.

3. *Valenciennes,*—an irregular hexagonal mesh, formed of two threads, partly twisted and platted at the top of the mesh. The pattern is worked in the net, similar to Mechlin lace.

4. *Lisle,*—a diamond mesh, formed of two threads platted to a pillar.

5. *Alençon,* (called *Blonde*),—hexagon of two threads, twisted similar to Buckingham lace, considered the most inferior of any made on the cushion.

5. *Alançon Point*,—formed of two threads to a pillar, with octagon and square meshes alternately.

The principal places where lace is made in the Netherlands, are Antwerp, Brussels, Mechlin, Louvain, Ghent, Valenciennes, and Lisle. It is also made at Chantilly, near Paris, (celebrated for veils), Charleville, Sedan, Le Comté de Bourgoyne, Dieppe, Havre, Harfleur, Pont l'Eveque, Gosom, Fécamp, Caen, Arras, Bapaume, &c., in France; and at various places in Spain, Portugal, and Italy.

Brussels Lace.—A notion of the extreme delicacy of the thread used, may be formed from the fact, that a pound of such thread sometimes costs 3,800 francs (£160), and that, with all the extra care bestowed upon it, it is even then not sufficiently refined for entire use, but that nearly one-half of the costly article is wasted. The extreme of this fine quality is the production of thread which cannot be worked when the wind is in the north, or the slightest breath of air moves, from its extraordinary tenuity.

Linen thread is thus obtained, worth more than six times its weight in pure gold; affording a striking exemplification of the manner in which labour imparts value to raw material. At the Brussels exhibition, an exquisite handkerchief, covered with the richest designs, was exhibited, made of the costly thread above mentioned,—a thread so gossamer-like, that a single filament was scarcely visible, even when backed by a blue ground. It takes sometimes three weeks to make a Flemish ell of Mechlin lace, and 400 bobbins are used for a lace three inches wide. For the Valenciennes lace, 250 bobbins are used in making an inch wide lace, and it takes six weeks to make an ell. Lace of three inches wide, will cost £10 the Flemish ell.

The adaptation of the stocking frame to the production of fancy work, and imitations of pillow lace, has created a new era in the lace manufacture of our country. The great improvement, however, which gave to this new branch of industry its most extraordinary impulse, resulted from the inventive ingenuity of Mr. Heathcoat. This gentleman, (formerly a mechanic, at Nottingham, and now, to his honour be it spoken, M.P. for Tiverton), constructed a machine, which, from certain arrangements of its parts, was called a "bobbin frame or machine," and hence has resulted the term *bobbin-net.* Some idea of the extraordinary changes which have resulted in the prices of the finished articles may be formed, when it is mentioned that lace, which was sold by Mr. Heathcoat, for five guineas per yard, soon after the taking out of his patent, can now be equalled, if not excelled, at eighteen-pence per yard; and that a certain width of net, which brought £17 per piece, twenty years ago, is now sold for seven shillings. It is impossible to give by means of a written description,

such an account of the lace machine as would be satisfactory; fortunately,
however, this is not necessary, as one, if not more, of the most recently-
improved machines, will be shown in full operation at the Exhibition.
The plain net having been produced, undergoes the process of "gassing"
or singeing, by means of gas, in order to remove the hairy filaments of
cotton remaining on the surface. If the net is to be embroidered by hand,
the pattern to be worked is stamped with some coloured pigment on the
net, and transferred to the "lace runner," as the embroideress is called.
Each workwoman has a frame, on which the net is stretched out horizontally, at a height of about three feet from the ground. She sits on a stool
or chair, places her left hand under the stretched net, to keep it in a right
position for working, and with her right hand works the pattern with
needle and thread, in every part where the stamper has imprinted a device.
The needle is inserted between and among the meshes of the net, and
stitches of greater or less length taken, until there is a body of thread
laid in, sufficient to mark the device conspicuously. This working round
of the outline is called "running," while the filling-up of the interior
parts, is termed either "fining" or "open-working," according as the
original meshes of the net are brought to a smaller or larger size by the
action of the needle.

Some of the articles in lace are decorated by "tambouring," instead of
"lace-running." This is done in frames similar to the others, and by
females in a similar rank of life, but a very small hook is used instead of a
needle, by which a thread is wound as a kind of chain about and among the
threads of the net. After the lace-runners have worked the collar, cape,
veil, or other net lace article, it is taken back to the manufacturer, who
then employs "lace menders" to examine every piece, and mend, with
needle and thread, every defective mesh in the net, whether produced in
the machine, or by any subsequent accident. This is done so skilfully, and
the form of the mesh so closely imitated, that the mended part can scarcely
be detected, except by a practised eye. The females engaged at "lace-
mending," earn much higher wages than the lace runners, on account of
the greater skill required. The net in lace is then bleached, and if required,
dyed black, after which it is dressed, rolled, pressed, and ticketed for sale.
As in some varieties there is a combination of hand-labour and machinery
to produce the pattern, we will briefly enumerate the principal kinds. In
"plain net," the whole fabric is made at the machine; in "sprigged net,"
the ground work, and a portion of every sprig are made at the machine,
and the outline of every sprig is then worked by hand. In "fancy broad-
net," the device as well as the ground-work are made at the machine. In
"plait-net," the same thing is observable, and also in "totting-net." In

"edging," and lace for borders, the device is now very generally worked by the machine; but in some varieties it is partly put in by hand; in "piece-goods," such as capes, collars, and veils, the device is almost wholly worked by hand, a very small proportion being effected by the Jacquard appendage to the lace machine.

A new lace machine is exhibited by Mr Birkin, of Nottingham. This machine is constructed upon the lever principle, and has extraordinary speed, being calculated, when in full operation, to accomplish about 130 motions a minute. The carcass, which is of cast iron, was produced by Messrs Keyton and Savage, of New Lenton, though the machine, in its completeness, has been built on Mr. Birkin's own premises, at Basford; its value is upwards of £600. The Jacquard apparatus is on the Manchester principle, and contains several new adaptations to the production of fresh patterns.

In 1850, 114,095,554 yards of cotton lace and patent net were exported, of the value of £563,533; and of thread-lace 468,166, of the value of £14,735; in the same year there was imported thread-lace, and cushion or pillow lace, to the value of £30,857; and embroidery and needlework, of the value of £146,198 imported, and £60,972 exported.

The bobbin-net trade of France occupies large manufactories at Calais, Lille, Douai, Cambrai, St. Quentin, Lyons, Caen, and Grand Couronne (Seine Inferieure). It is calculated that this branch of industry employs 1,500 machines, and 4,500 persons. The consumption of tulle is considerable in France. The export of thread and cotton lace amounts to £140,000. The tulle, blonde, and bobbin-net trade of Lyons employ also 200 looms, producing an annual value of nearly £80,000; 130 looms are employed in the manufacture of lace gloves. The value of the manufacture of these different kinds of lace together, is estimated at more than £400,000 per annum; the export of silk lace alone is valued at £20,000. Thread and cotton lace, the production of Lille, Caen, Bayeux, Alençon, Honfleur, Dieppe, Valenciennes, Arras, Puy, Mirecourt, &c., of the value of £115,000 are annually exported.

It is difficult to ascertain the present value of the lace manufacture of the United Kingdom. We believe, however, that the value of the pillow lace trade of England is about £150,000, giving employment to 30,000 persons; that of the machine lace trade to £3,000,000, affording employment to 15,000 persons; whilst the Irish lace trade may be estimated at £22,000, and 1,000 hands. The total value would thus amount to upwards of £3,170,000.

IRISH LACE.

Messrs. Lambert and Bury, of Limerick, exhibit the following specimens of the capabilities of the Irish Lace Girls.

Richly shaded Lace Flounce,—measuring 5¼ yards long, 31 inches deep.

Richly shaded Lace Shawl,—measuring 2¼ yards square.

Richly worked Scarf à la mode de Valenciennes,—measuring 1 yard wide, 3¼ yards long.

Richly shaded Lace Dress.

THE tambouring of net and ornamental lace work, was not known in Ireland, before the year 1829, when it was introduced, and a factory formed in the city of Limerick, by the late Mr. Charles Walker, Mr. Lambert's former partner.

The original establishment continues in full operation. Messrs. Lambert and Bury now employ between five and six hundred pair of hands in the various departments of this beautiful branch of female ingenuity and industry, producing most chaste, elegant, and elaborate designs of British lace dresses, shawls, veils, &c. &c.

Messrs. Lambert and Co. send twice every week to their warehouse in London, the productions of their Limerick manufactory, which are sold exclusively to the wholesale houses,—and by them distributed to all parts of the united kingdom. The present facility and small cost of conveyance, enables the retail dealer in every town in the three kingdoms, to sell the Limerick lace, equally as reasonable as it can be purchased in the city where it is manufactured. The demand has so increased of late, that the proprietors have been adding from fifty to one hundred hands yearly,—and all the persons in their employ have work summer and winter.

In the city and suburbs of Limerick, there are upwards of 1,000 women and children employed at this trade, maintaining themselves, and their families, amounting to three or four thousand persons.

The *Gold Isis Medal* of the Society of Arts, was awarded to Messrs. Lambert and Bury, for their tamboured lace, in 1850; and in the same year the Royal Dublin Society, at their triennial Exhibition of Arts and Manufactures, acknowledged their sense of the value and importance of Messrs. Lambert and Co.'s efforts in promoting the welfare of the Irish population, as well as the skill and taste developed in the productions of their manufactory, by awarding them one of the Society's "gold medals."

We wish to call especial attention to the following specimens of domestic Irish manufacture, exhibited by the Irish Work Society of Regent-street, London.

Specimens of Appliquée* Lace, imitation of Brussels, from Currah Chase, County Limerick.

This manufacture was established by the Dowager Lady de Vere, and is now carried on by the present Lady de Vere, with great success; large quantities have been sold in London. It is an imitation of Brussels and Honiton lace, at one half the price; it washes extremely well, and is very durable.

Specimens of the same from the Marquis of Bath's Estate, under the direction of Tresham Kennedy, Esq.—In the schools established under this gentleman's care, large quantities of this lace have been made, and almost any quantity could be produced, if there were a certain market for the article.

Specimens of Crochet, novel and cheap imitation of Guipure.—This is a new manufacture within the last three years, and has succeeded extremely well. It is extensively made in nearly all parts of Ireland, and is used for curtains, chair covers, articles of dress, and furniture. The cost of these specimens is about one fourth of the original.

Trimming and Collars of real Guipure made from old models.—This is the first time that the old guipure has been successfully copied. This is made in thread by poor women in their cottages, and is a remarkable production, as it does not vary from the originals in any particular.

Specimens of Straw Plait.—Straw plaiting is done in many parts of Ireland, but is not a flourishing trade in consequence of the demand being small; the leghorn and tuscan plaits are made of Irish grasses, collected by the poor women who sell this plait, at from 1s. to 2s. 6d. per score.

Tabinets or Poplins, from Mrs. Moran, Dublin.—Mrs. Moran obtained the prize at the Dublin Society's show last year. The poplins are made of various degrees of richness, from 3s. 4d., to 5s. 6d. per yard, retail price. They are also made for furniture of a richer and thicker description, from 7s. upwards. They are superior to the English tabouret furniture, which, being composed of cotton and silk, is liable to fade; while the tabinets are not, being composed of worsted and silk. Any design for furniture would be made to order, and the Irish Work Society have a large stock of poplins for sale, the same qualities as those exhibited.

Specimens of Pillow Lace.—This is a manufacture rapidly increasing in Ireland, and one of the few, where the supply cannot equal the demand.

* This term is used to express any kind of lace, the ground of which being machine-wrought, the ornamentation made on the pillow, and afterwards applied to the ground.

Black Silk Mittens,—Imitated from the Maltese; which they excel in fineness.

Specimens of fine Knitting.—There is no kind of work in which the poor women and children excel more than in this, which has been brought to an extraordinary degree of perfection, almost equal to fine pillow lace. The baby's cap valued at 15s., is a curious specimen of this work. Very young children will knit with a surprising degree of precision and nicety; and there is scarcely a part of Ireland where this is not understood and practised.

Specimens of White Wool Mats, superior in durability, thickness, and whiteness, to the usual wool rugs, and also cheaper. The wool is stripped off the skin, dressed and picked; the best is chosen and sewn on linen. They wear for *many years,* and wash with the greatest ease.

Specimens of Muslin Imitation of Guipure.—These are from Carrickmacross, where there are several schools, and a considerable number of poor women employed in this work, for which there is a full demand.

Specimens of Embroidery "Au Blanc."—The peculiarity of these embroideries consists in their being worked, and shown for sale, unwashed, as it comes from the hands of the workers, and is a beautiful specimen of the industry, care, and cleanliness of the poor girls and women, under the most unfavourable circumstances of smoky cottages and poverty.

Specimens of Plain Work from various localities, Shirts, &c.—The Irish peasantry excel in plain work, and shirt making. The beauty of these specimens cannot be surpassed, and their cheapness is a great merit. The Irish Work Society can supply fine linen shirts, like the specimen, at 12s. each, and with rather less stitching, at 10s. 6d.; and can execute orders for baby linen, and all plain work, in equally good style and moderate prices.

Specimens of Woollen Hosiery.—These have been chosen of various qualities, from many different localities in Ireland; the prices of the socks varying from 9s. per dozen; and the stockings, from 15s. The Irish peasantry excel in the knitting of every sort of woollen, cotton, and thread hosiery, and can produce them at a price to compete with that of woven goods. The Irish Work Society exhibit, besides the above coarser articles, some of the finest thread and cotton, in black and white; also finest lambs-wool, lace, and plain socks and hose; but it is impossible to give a sufficient idea in our limited space of what can be done in these goods. The largest orders could be easily executed, and the Society would undertake to supply any quantity of these specimens. There is also a specimen of knitted Jersey, much approved for yachting, hunting, &c.

Specimens of Balbriggan Woven Cotton Hosiery.—These are from Smyth's Hosiery Factory, George's Hill, Balbriggan. There is no hosiery equal to this for softness, elasticity, and durability. They are made in all qualities, from 1s. to 10s. 6d.; all equally good of their kind. Large quantities of *imitation* Balbriggan stockings are sold in London, but none are equal to the original. Mr. Smyth has gone to considerable expense of late years, to improve his machinery, enlarge his factory, and increase the number of his workpeople, who will not readily forget the extraordinary kindness of their employer, during the trial period of famine in Ireland. The first class medal was awarded to Mr. Smyth, at each of the Dublin Society's Triennial Exhibitions; on the last occasion, a gold medal was given for *continued* improvement. The Queen has been pleased to appoint Messrs. Smyth "Hosiers to Her Majesty."

Specimens of Bog Oak Carving.—These are made from the oak found in the bogs, and which has become black from the effects of time and immersion. At Killarney, every sort of furniture is made from the bog oak, yew, and fir; and also from the arbutus, which abounds there. The Irish diamond is introduced into the ornaments exhibited here.

ALPACA UMBRELLAS AND PARASOLS.

In our notice of the woollen manufacture, we mentioned the introduction of the wool of the Alpaca sheep of South America into our manufactures. Bradford in Yorkshire, is the principal place where the various fabrics are made, either of Alpaca wool alone, or of the wool mixed with other textile substances, as silk, &c. The Alpaca wool appears to occupy a place between ordinary sheep's wool and silk, and the fabric manufactured from it, is therefore remarkably well adapted for umbrellas, to which purpose Messrs. Sangsters, of 75, Cheapside, have patented its application.

Nearly three years have now elapsed since letters patent were taken out for the application of Alpaca to umbrellas. The idea was suggested by the fact, that it had been long used as a substitute for silk in many articles, where cheapness and durability were required. The result of the experiment has more than borne out the anticipation the patentees then formed of its adaptation to their trade, upwards of 60,000 umbrellas, and 25,000 parasols, made of this material, having been sold in little more than two years, whilst the demand for it still increasing, proves that its advantages are appreciated proportion as they become known.

This fact is the more gratifying, as (in addition to the obstacles thrown in the way of all who introduce an improvement, from the prejudices of some manufacturers in the same trade) in consequence of the price of silk having fallen in 1848 nearly 50 per cent, a cheap umbrella of that material was sold at a price unusually low; but silk having risen to its former value, a best umbrella cannot now be sold at less than double the price of an Alpaca.

Cashmere Shawls.—The shawl manufacture is believed to have originated in the valley of Cashmere, the ancient Caspira in the north-west of India. Though not so flourishing as it once was, the manufacture is still prosecuted in this province to a very considerable extent. The shawls are the very best that are made, possessing unequalled firmness, delicacy and warmth. They are formed of the inner hair of a variety of the common goat, reared on the cold dry table land of Thibet, elevated from 14,000 to 16,000 feet above the level of the sea. The inner or fine wool is covered over and protected by a quantity of long shaggy hair, which is, of course, carefully separated from it before it is manufactured. The genuine shawl wool has been imported into this country; and the fairest Edinburgh and Paisley shawls have been produced from it. But it must be admitted, that shawls have nowhere been made that can come, as respects quality, into successful competition with those of Cashmere. Even those made at Delhi and Lahore by native Cashmerians, employing the same material, are wanting in fineness, and have a degenerate coarse appearance. The superiority of the shawls manufactured at Cashmere, is by some ascribed to the quality of the water, but it is most probably owing to a variety of circumstances, which, though each may appear of little importance, collectively give a character to the manufacture.

About £450,000 to £500,000 worth of shawls are annually exported from Paris, Lyons, Nîmes, Rouen, Amiens, and St. Quentin, and a larger amount is disposed of in the home trade.

Messrs. Clabburn, of Norwich, exhibits two patterns of Cashmere shawls, in longs and squares, of various colours, and some also made in all silk. This is the first attempt in Norwich to weave figured shawls in a Jacquard loom on this new principle. Shawl mufflers for gentlemen. They were made on the new principle of Jacquard loom. Linderine check shawls, a make peculiar to this firm, exhibited on account of their cheapness; all silk spun long shawls; Alhambra long silks shawl; fancy check shawl, made in silk and wool; rich brocade Jacquard poplin, made upon a new principle; specimens of Chêni poplins, in robes à bordures, coverd with figures; Jacquard robes à bordures, made in silk warp, and wefted with China grass—each side shewing a perfect figure, and having the effect of needle work; robes à bordures, Jacquard silk brocade figure, upon mixed grounds; and some Ballano lustres.

CARPET MANUFACTURE.

Fabrication de Tapis.   Teppish Manufactur.

THE carpet manufacture of this country is not of any ancient date, and the use of carpets up to the middle of the last century was so very limited, that as a manufacture, it occupied a very subordinate rank. With the increasing wealth of the country, the carpet manufacture has steadily increased, and thus this article of domestic comfort, which, only a few generations since, was but occasionally found in the mansions of the rich, has now become a part of the furniture of almost every house.

The principal kinds of carpeting manufactured in this country, are— Axminster, Patent Axminster, Wilton or Velvet Pile, Brussels, Patent Tapestry, Scotch or Kidderminster, and Venetian or Dutch.

Axminster carpets derive their name from a town in Devonshire, where the manufacture was originally established in England. About 20 years since the carpet trade was given up at Axminster, and the looms removed to Wilton, at which place it is still carrried on by Messrs. Blackmore, Brothers. A few years since, the manufacture of these carpets was commencd in London, by Messrs. Jackson and Graham, of Oxford-street, who produce carpets of the largest dimensions, in one piece. This is the only carpet manufactory in the metropolis. The principle of the manufacture, is precisely the same as that of the Turkey and Persian carpets, (which continue to be imported into this country), and similar to the *haute laine* or "high pile" of the Gobelins manufactory at Paris, and those of Aubusson and Tournay. The designs, the colours, and the texture of these carpets are much more beautiful than the Turkey, and rival the best productions of the French and Belgian looms.

The warp and weft, or as they are more commonly called, chain and shoot, are generally both of linen, which are altogether concealed from the upper surface, by the tufts of worsted or wool tied to, or fastened under, and round the warp. The process is a tedious one, and the first cost of these carpets is, consequently, very expensive, but their durability amply compensates.

There are but two manufactories in England, one at Wilton, and one in London, that of Messrs. Jackson and Graham.

Patent Axminster.—These carpets, and also rugs, are manufactured extensively at Glasgow, by the patentees, Messrs. Templeton and Co. The object of the invention was to give the beautiful appearance of real Axminster, at less cost, the pile being woven in the first instance, as chenille, and by an ingenious process, cut into strips, and re-woven with a thick back of hemp or jute.

The economy consists in making a great number of carpets or rugs of the same design : the first weaving being the same cost for one, as for any number up to thirty-six, or even more.

Wilton, or velvet pile, and Brussel carpets, are all woven on the same principle, the difference being, that in Brussels, the wire, by which the pile is raised, is drawn out, and in velvet, cut out by a knife. The pattern is formed by having frames of worsted on bobbins, placed over each other, each having, for the usual width, 260 threads, the threads in each frame being of different colours, and some of the frames striped with more than one colour, when the design to be executed requires it, as in flower patterns. By the aid of the Jacquard machine, now generally applied to Brussels carpet looms, the threads are drawn up to form the pattern, the inner part under, and then they are drawn down over it, and a shoot of linen passed across to bind the surface, and another across the back. The chain or warp forming the back is always of linen, as well as the shoot. The number of colours, or shades of colour, that can be used in a line, is limited to the number of frames of worsted, which rarely exceed five, although some few looms have six or seven ; and additional shades are obtained by striping or planting, as before mentioned.

Patent tapestry carpets have, like the Brussels, a terry or velvet surface, as the wire may be drawn or cut out : and the number of shades that can be obtained, may be said to be almost unlimited, by which means greater scope is afforded for the execution of designs with flower or coloured scrolls. There is, in addition, great economy of worsted, one frame, or rather beam, 260 threads, (only being used for the ordinary width,) all of which works upon the surface, and instead of the other frames used in Brussels carpets, what is called a stuffing-chain, or warp of linen or cotton, is made to supply their place, and being a much cheaper material than worsted, a great saving in cost is effected. The pattern is formed by printing or colouring each of the 260 threads separately, at spaces with the various shades as they follow each other in the design; so that when the ends are placed together in succession, they form a warp, with the design elongated to the extent, that the wire over which it is passed, takes it up in weaving, and reduces it in the carpet to the proportions of the design. The process is beautifully simple and ingenious, but requires much care in placing and arranging the threads. It was invented and patented by Mr. Whytock, of Edinburgh, about 19 years since, and is now the most flourishing branch of the carpet manufacture.

Venetian and Dutch carpets are made in a common loom, with worsted or woollen warps; the shoot being of linen, woollen, cotton, or mixed material, by which means it is produced at a low price, and is chiefly used for bedrooms. Kidderminster or Scotch carpet, is made with two or three warps of different colours, (in the latter case it is called thin ply,) and with shoot of woollen; some times of many different colours, each colour requiring a separate shuttle. This description of carpeting is made extensively in America by looms to which steam power has been applied.

Steam power has recently been applied to weaving Brussels carpets, without the aid of a wire, with a plain surface, which is afterwards printed, by which means the patent tapestry carpets are closely imitated. This loom is the invention of Mr. Sievier, and the machine by which they are printed, the invention of Mr. Burch ; the manufacture being carried on at Rochdale.

A loom has recently been invented and patented by Mr. Wm. Wood, for weaving the same description of carpeting, with a wire for adding a thick back of some cheap material, so that great thickness and softness can be obtained at little cost.

The latter invention has been successfully and extensively applied to the manufacture of rugs, by Mr. Whytock's successors (Messrs. Henderson and Wednell), at Lassevade, near Edinburgh.

The French have always been prominent in the eyes of Europe, for the perfection they have attained in the manufacture of the highest descriptions of carpets, tapestries, wall-hangings, and all articles of a similar nature. It must, however, be borne in mind, that they were the first in the field, and that the patronage of a luxurious Monarchy, in the midst of aristocratic imitators, had a favourable influence on this interesting and necessary branch, previous to the revolution. Since that time a similar result has been attained by different means. Improved taste for design, the encouragement given to the study of chemistry, and the necessity for economy, have each contributed to further the manufacture of such works as are produced at the present day, and which, in many respects, rival the best performances of the period of Louis XIV.

The principal seat of the carpet manufacture in France, is Aubusson, but a large establishment has sprung up within a few years at Turcoing, where moquette or velvet pile carpets, of a very beautiful description, are made, as also a fine description for covering sofas and chairs. The manufacture is increasing in France, and would, no doubt, make much more rapid progress if exposed to competition ; but the duty on carpets imported is almost prohibitory, being levied by weight, and amounting to from 60 to 70 per cent.

We have no data enabling us to ascertain the quantity of carpets annually made in this country; we believe the number of looms to be rather more than 5,000, and the value of carpets manufactured to be about £1,500,000. Our principal export of carpets is to the United States of America, British North America, South America, and the continent of Europe, the quantity exported in 1849, being 1,565,745 yards. Most of the Brussels carpets are made at Kidderminster, and the Kidderminster or Scotch, in Scotland and the North of England.

The carpet manufactures of Aubusson, Felleton, Turcoing, Nîmes, Abbeville, and the Gobelins, produce an annual value of £320,000.

FELTED CLOTH MANUFACTURE.

About ten years since a new manufacture, which has now risen to some degree of eminence, was introduced into this country ; this was the manufacture of woollen and other fabrics, of which wool and fur form the principal component parts ; the term felts or felted goods being applied to the article so manufactured. This felted cloth or other fabric, is produced without the processes of spinning and weaving, by laying the fibres of loose, scribbled, or carded wool, or other material, capable of felting, in a thick sheet or bat of suitable length and thickness, for forming commercial ends or lengths of cloth, which is afterwards hardened, and milled or fulled, and thereby converted into a felt or felted cloth.

The fabric or manufactured article thus produced, depends wholly for its union and strength upon the principle or tendency of these animal products when properly treated, to combine and unite, or, as it is commonly called, to felt together without the usual auxiliaries of spinning and weaving, or the use of any adhesive mixtures.

The goods manufactured by this felting process, may be subjected to any, or all of the different processes of raising, shearing, or cropping, boiling, pressing, &c., used by manufacturers on the old system of woven cloth.

The felted cloth is peculiarly applicable for carpets, table-coverings, window-curtains, cloths of various descriptions, and many other useful purposes.

And as the richest colours and most tasteful designs can readily be transferred to its surface, by means of suitable printing machinery, this new branch of industry is rapidly advancing in public estimation, and the immense economy in price, and the great durability of the fabric, gives it additional claims to encouragement and support.

This new fabric is the subject of a patent, being manufactured exclusively by the Victoria Felt Company, of Love-lane, Wood-street, Cheapside. The specimens of this manufacture exhibited, well deserve the notice of the visitor.

MANUFACTURES IN FUR, LEATHER, HAIR, &c.

Fourrures, Cuirs, Orins, &c.

THE visitors to the Exhibition, expecially those of the gentler sex, whilst admiring the unique display of furs exhibited by Mr. Nicolay, will, perhaps, be somewhat startled when they are informed of the prodigious number of skins, of various animals, annually imported into this country, and manufactured into various articles of ornament, utility, and comfort. The following is a list of skins imported in 1849:—Bear-skins, 9,872; beaver, 33,756; cat, 4,334; coney, 144,890; ermine, 187,104; fitch, 65,091; fox, 74,602; lynx, 45,953; marten, 223,117; mink, 189,362; musquash, 907,407; nutria, 3,768; otter, 13,961; racoon, 488,736; squirrel, or calabar, 2,215,928. Large quantities of some of these were re-exported to other parts of the globe; the ermine, squirrel, marten, and musquash, being entirely, or for the most part, retained for home use, in addition to large numbers of the other furs.

British North America furnishes us with the largest number of bear, beaver, marten, musquash, otter, and seal skins. From the United States chiefly, we import mink, deer, and goat skins; from Buenos Ayres, nutria; our supplies of lamb skin is chiefly from Italy; of fitch from Germany, Belgium, and France; of undressed kid from Tuscany, Italy, and British India; goat from Holland, Cape of Good Hope, and British India; whilst of dressed kid, by far the greatest quantity imported comes from France.

The leather manufactures of Bermondsey, Bristol, &c., are represented at the Exhibition, and evidence afforded of improvements in the manufacture of ornamented, embossed, stamped, and varnished leathers. We have no information before us as to the quantity of leather annually manufactured in this kingdom. The following particulars will serve to give some idea of our trade with other countries in leather and articles manufactured therefrom:

In addition to the skins enumerated under the account of furs, there were imported, in 1849, 38,750 deer skins; 256,897 goat; 107,450 kid; dressed kid, 220,796; undressed lamb skins, 1,800,824; dressed or tanned lamb skins, 8,715; 470,834 seal skins; and 287,458 sheep skins. Of the three former, a large quantity were re-exported, but the principal bulk of the remainder retained for home use.

There were imported, in 1850, of untanned hides, dry, 150,575 cwts, and 83,799 cwts. re-exported; wet, 441,345 cwts., and 29,778 cwts. re-exported. Of tanned, tawed, curried, or dressed (except Russia hides), 1,876,232 lbs., of which 105,570 lbs. were re-exported. Of leather manufactures, there were imported 22,346 pairs of womens' boots and calashes, of which 19,776 pairs were entered for home consumption; 4,856 pairs of womens' shoes, with cork or double soles, quilted shoes or clogs, of which 4,780 pairs were entered for home consumption; 114,564 pairs of womens' shoes, of silk, satin, stuff, or leather, of which 103,774 were entered for home consumption; 34,178 pairs of mens' boots and shoes, of which 24,595 pairs were entered for home consumption; 1,698 pairs of other sorts (children's), of which 529 pairs were entered for home consumption; and 603,802 pairs of boot fronts, of which 600,358 were entered for home consumption. Of gloves there were imported, 3,261,061 pairs, of which 2,849,275 pairs were entered for home consumption, and 401,009 pairs exported. Of manufactures of leather, not particularly enumerated, to the value of £5,289, of which £3,928 were entered for home consumption.

Of British and Irish produce, there were exported, in 1850, 32,112 cwts. of unwrought leather, of the declared value of £181,976. Of gloves, 31,770 lbs., of the value of £18,821. Of wrought leather of other sorts, 1,617,292 lbs., of the value of £283,911; and of saddlery and harness, to the value of £123,948.

Brazil and the Argentine Republic supplies the principal portion of untanned hides imported; and France, boots, shoes, and gloves. Our principal exports of leather are to the United States, the British West India Islands, British North America, and Australia: the latter of which, and British territories in India, are our best customers for saddlery and harness. The boot and shoe trade still continues the staple trade of Northampton; upwards of 30,000 pairs per week being there manufactured.

The total annual value of the leather trade of France is estimated at £1,000,000. Paris, Grenoble, Niort, and Vendôme, are the great centres of the glove manufacture, which employs a large number of work-people, particularly of women, in the country. The export of leather gloves is valued at £400,000 per annum.

The manufacture of embossed leathers, ornamented with gold, silver, and various colours, was formerly carried on to a considerable extent in Spain, Italy, and Flanders. At a later date, Germany, France, and England held the first place in the production of those embossed and ornamented leathers, which, from the distinct relief obtainable, and the brilliancy of colour of which the leather was susceptible, and resistance to damp offered by the material, rendered those productions peculiarly fitted for panels and hangings. The manufacture of these leather tapestries, which appears to have been discontinued in England during the last sixty or seventy years, has been revived by Mr. Leake, and our readers will do well to examine with care and attention the specimens at the Exhibition.

We must not omit to say a few words on the manufacture of hair-seating, a branch of trade chiefly carried on at Sheffield and Worcester. The long-flowing manes and tails, of the horses which roam wildly over the plains of South America, and other places, are first " willowed," as mentioned under the linen and cotton manufactures, then combed, sorted into regular lengths, and dyed a jet-black colour: they are now ready for the loom. For weaving the hair-seating, the ordinary loom is employed, the chain or warp being either of cotton or linen, coloured black, by means of the size applied to it. A single hair is fixed to the shuttle, which is thrown in the usual manner. As the horse-hair is in single lengths, and not capable of being joined, an attendant on the weaver attaches a hair to the shuttle each time it passes the loom, and as the hair used is a little longer than the width of the material fabricated, the ends are cut off evenly, when the weaving is completed. The woven fabric is then hot-pressed. The introduction of the jacquard-loom has enabled the manufacturer to produce handsome patterns of figured horse-hair seating. Messrs. Samuel Laycock and Sons, of Sheffield, and Messrs. Webb, of Worcester, exhibit some fine specimens of this manufacture.

COCOA-NUT MATTING, RUGS, &c.

THE utility of the husk of the cocoa-nut is derived from its tough fibrous character. From the commencement, the husk is worked up in a damp state; it is thrown into water, where it soaks and swells, and the fibres develope themselves. It is then passed between two pairs of rollers, of different diameters, and thus torn and crushed. It is then opened, and in that state remitted to the water. The material is now brought to a mill, having rollers armed with spikes, revolving with a high velocity, and by this means the fibre is combed out. A refuse matter, of an adhesive spongy character, is now separated, which, having the power in an eminent degree of retaining moisture, has been lately successfully applied as a manure to dry soils. The fibres are now combed until they are straight, by a set of rollers having their teeth set on an elastic surface. The fibre is now sorted into three qualities. The finest is used for stuffing cushions, sofas, and mattrasses; the second is employed in the manufacture of matting, and other similar objects; the third is a stiff, bristly fibre, of which brushes are manufactured, in the same manner as bristles. For brushes, intended to be applied to animal fibre, as hair, woollens, &c., a vegetable fibre is peculiarly suitable, from the tendency of animal fibres to combine, whenever they are brought together. Hammocks, with mattrasses worked in with them, are made of the cocoa-nut fibre, and are esteemed for their cleanliness, admitting of being washed with great facility, and being exempt from the presence of insects, to which the fibre is inimical. Mr. Treloar, of Ludgate Hill, is the principal exhibitor in this department.

MANUFACTURES IN INDIA-RUBBER, VULCANIZED INDIA-RUBBER, AND GUTTA PERCHA.

INDIA-RUBBER.

In addition to its application as a waterproofing agent, the visitor will notice a great variety of purposes to which this vegetable exudation has been successfully applied, especially in the manufacture of numerous kinds of hosiery articles, small wares, &c., the produce of Leicester, Manchester, &c. Its elasticity is its great recommendation, thus enabling it to maintain its ground in public use, without fear of being supplanted by its non-elastic competitor, gutta-percha. Messrs. Bedells, of Leicester, Mr. Westhead, of Manchester, and other manufacturers, have been successful in making useful applications of the elastic property of india-rubber, in the manufacture of various articles of dress, gloves, &c.

Vulcanized India-Rubber.—In the form of vulcanized india-rubber, or india-rubber combined with sulphur, Mr. Hancock has succeeded in effecting a great variety of useful applications of this substance to purposes, for which, in its unprepared state, it was inapplicable. The combination of

[sulphur with the india-rubber, whilst it does not interfere with its elastic and waterproofing capabilities, prevents the rigidity which india-rubber itself acquires, when exposed to changes of temperature. Vulcanized india-ruubber thus becomes admirably adapted for the manufacture of hose for the conveyance of hot or cold water, as for fire and garden engines, &c Mr. Hancock has also successfully applied it to the construction of portable baths, for which purpose it succeeds admirably. In addition to the various articles exhibited by Mr. Hancock, illustrative of the useful application of vulcanized india-rubber, we may mention the construction of a gasometer of this material, for a gas works in Mexico, which has recently been forwarded to that country.

GUTTA PERCHA.

This useful article has now become so extensively employed for commercial and domestic purposes, that a few remarks on it may not be uninteresting to the visitor, in his examination of the almost endless variety of articles manufactured therefrom, exhibited by the Gutta-Percha Company. Gutta-percha is the concrete juice of a large tree of the same name, abounding in Borneo, &c., and is obtained by periodical tapping of the tree. The introduction of it into this country, is due to Dr. Montgomery, in 1843, when its qualities having been carefully examined, it was soon found

applicable to a great variety of useful purposes. It is imported into this
country in large blocks; and so much has the demand for articles manufactured therefrom increased, that hundreds of tons per annum are now
imported. In manufacturing the rough gutta-percha into articles of utility,
the blocks are first cut into slices, by means of a cutting-machine formed of

a circular iron plate, of about five feet in diameter, in which there are three
radical slots, furnished with as many knives or blades. The blocks are
placed in an inclined shoot, so as to present one end to the operation of the
cutters. The slices are then placed in a wooden tank, containing hot

water, in which they are left to soak until found in a plastic state. They are afterwards passed through a mincing-cylinder, similar to that used in paper-mills for the conversion of rags into pulp, and then thoroughly cleansed in cold water tanks; the water, in cases of impure gutta-percha, being mixed with a solution of common soda or chloride of lime. It is next put into a masticating-machine, such as is used in the manufacture of caoutchouc, and then pressed through rollers; thus being converted into sheets of various width and thickness. When necessary, the sheets are again masticated, and again passed through rollers. These sheets are subsequently cut into boards by vertical knives, placed at the further end of the table, along which the sheets are carried by a cloth or web to another roller, round which they pass, and are cut into the required widths. The bands or straps are then removed, and coiled up ready for use. Driving bands for machinery are thus made; and shoe-soles and heels are stamped out of similar sheets of gutta-percha. In making tubes or pipes, either of gutta-percha or any of its compounds, a mass of gutta-percha, after being thoroughly masticated, is placed in a metal cylinder furnished with a similar piston, by which it is pressed down into an air-box, kept hot with steam, which has at its lower end a number of perforations, through which the plastic material is forced into a cup, whence it passes out, round a core, into the desired tubular form, and thence through a gauge to the required size, and into a receiver of cold water, being drawn to the other end of a long trough by a cord passing round a pulley at the far end of the trough, and returning to the person in attendance on the machine, who gradually draws the pipe away from the air-machine. Thus, tubes of considerable length and diameter are made to a very great extent, and are used for the conveyance of water and other liquids. To enumerate the various useful purposes to which gutta-percha is applied, would occupy more space than we are able to devote to it; we would, therefore, direct the attention of the visitor to the varied articles exhibited by the Gutta Percha Company.

Elastic Grotesque Faces, imported from Germany, are cast in glue and treacle: the composition of which printing-ink rollers are made; gutta-percha is not elastic, and india-rubber is too elastic for the slow grave change of expression after a squeeze.

MANUFACTURE OF PLATE AND PLATED GOODS.

Fabrication de l'Argenterie et de la Vaisselle.

Manufactur von Selber, und Platterlen Waaren.

———

THE gorgeous display of gold and silver plate from the workshops of the metropolis,—and the taste, design, and skill, manifested in the articles exhibited,—will not fail to prove a source of great attraction to the visitor. It will require no further notice at our hands than can be given in a few figures, having reference to the production and consumption of the precious metals.

The increase in the quantity of gold obtained within the last ten years, has been very great. In 1840 the entire production of gold was estimated at £1,290,000; in 1848, by aid of the Ural Mountain Mines, it reached to had £4,160,000; and in 1850, by help of California, to £14,790,000.

The entire production of silver in 1840, was £6,852,274; in 1848, £6,867,237; and in 1850, to £7,610,000.

The quantity of gold and silver coin of all denominations, in all quarters of the globe, is set down by the best authorities, at from £300,000,000 to £400,000,000; and the quantity in plate and ornaments, at about £400,000,000 more. It is estimated that £5,400,000 are annually consumed in manufactures.

The number of ounces of gold and silver plate annually made and retained for home use in this country, is about 8,500 of gold, and 1,000,000 ounces of silver. In the year 1811, the amount was 7,333 ounces of gold, and 1,254,128 ounces of silver; whence it is evident that the quantity manufactured for home use, has not increased in any relative proportion to the increase of the population.

London is the seat of the manufacture of the gold, and of most of the silver plate. Sheffield occupies the second place: at the latter town about 4,000 lbs. weight of silver plate is annually assayed.

The manufacture of jewellry and trinkets in France, produces a consumption of about 10,000 lbs. weight of gold per annum, of the standard of $\frac{760}{1000}$, equal in value to about £500,000. The labour very nearly equals in value the cost of the gold, so that the total value reaches nearly to £1,000,000. The threefold industry of jewellery, gold and silver plate, and trinkets, is represented by an annual value of more than £2,000,000.

Plated Goods.—It has always been the case, that where people could not afford the real article, they have contrived a substitute, as much resembling it as possible. This remark is peculiarly applicable to plate: and various have been the methods from time to time employed to give the inferior metals the appearance of pure gold and silver. The art of overlaying one metal with another of greater value, is of great antiquity, the mode of accomplishing it being either by some process analogous to washing or gilding, or by fixing thin sheets and foils of the precious metals in some less adhesive manner. Next came the process of amalgamation, and what is called " French plating." In the first of these processes, a mixture of chloride of silver, sal-ammoniac, &c., is rubbed over the article to be coated, which is then exposed to a degree of heat sufficient to " cause the silver to run," when it is removed from the fire, and dipped in dilute muriatic acid, to clean it. In the case of the French plating, the practice is to make the metal very clean, heat it until nearly red-hot, when silver leaf is laid on, and immediately burnished down, the heat and friction causing it to adhere perfectly. By this method, successive layers of silver can be applied to any thickness the work may require. Another method is to cover the metal with a paste of chloride of silver, alum, and cream of tartar, and when well rubbed and polished, a layer of silver coating is obtained.

It was not, however, until 1742, that the present method of plating goods was practised. It was in that year that an ingenious mechanic of Sheffield, Mr. Thomas Bolsover, when employed to repair the handle of a knife which was composed partly of silver, and partly of copper, was struck with the possibility of uniting the two metals, so as to form a cheap substitute for silver. Mr. Hancock, of Sheffield, following out the suggestion of Bolsover, (who confined his discovery to the manufacture of some small articles,) next applied the process to the manufacture of candlesticks, teapots, &c., which previously had been formed only of wrought silver. Thus commenced the plated goods trade of Sheffield, which place stands, to the present day, unrivalled, both as regards the extent of the manufacture, and the elegance and durability of the articles produced. Birmingham is a competitor with Sheffield in the production of cheap and showy articles; but in quality, Sheffield stands alone. The silvering processes we have before mentionnd, were always performed *after* the articles were formed, but in the plating process of which we have last spoken, the copper is united to the silver *previous* to the formation of the articles required. The rolling of silver in contact with the inferior metals is performed by extensive and powerful mills in London, Sheffield, and Birmingham; but the largest portion, as regards the extent of surface, is executed at Birmingham. The plate of the respectable Sheffield houses contains more than five pennyweights of

H

silver to the pound of copper or other metal employed, whilst much of the Birmingham plate contains but three pennyweights to the pound. Much of this low quality metal is also sent from Birmingham to Sheffield to be manufactured, to the injury of the respectable Sheffield trade.

Much of the Sheffield plate is plated on both sides, besides which, the small beading which surrounds the edges of the plated goods is formed of silver alone.

The introduction of German silver and other metallic alloys, of a white colour, has led to their substitution to some extent for copper, in the manufacture of plated goods : so that when the surface of silver wears away, its disappearance is not so readily perceived as when copper forms the basis of the article.

Our manufactures of plated goods have an advantage over all others, from the perfection of the machinery used in this country, for rolling metals. The difference thus caused, if estimated in money value, is in favour of the English manufactures, as compared with those of France, in the proportion of 17 to 13 in the cost of the material employed. It was estimated some few years since, that the value of articles of this manufacture used in the United Kingdom, amounts to £1,200,000 per annum ; while in France the consumption does not exceed £40,000 per annum: an equal value being also exported from that country, principally to Holland, Belgium, Spain, the Sardinian States, Germany, Mexico, and the United States of America.

We now come to notice the new process of gilding and silvering, by means of voltaic electricity, which, in the hands of Elkington and others, forms a new feature in the plating trade of this and other countries. This process is founded on the principle, that if a voltaic current be passed through a vessel containing a metallic solution, the metal becomes separated from the liquid, and deposited in a solid form. Thus, if we wish to coat a metal with silver, we proceed as follows :—

The prepared articles, when quite cleansed at the surface, are immersed in tanks containing a chemical solution of silver. The mode of immersing them is curious ; metallic rods cross the tanks from side to side, and from these the various articles are suspended by wires temporarily affixed to them. Spoons, forks, plates, salvers, cups, caudlesticks, candelabra, and a countless assemblage of other articles, are thus suspended side by side, but without being in contact ; the general arrangement of the tank, as to the placing of the wires, &c., being regulated according to the kind of articles to be coated. A galvanic current, derived from an apparatus near at hand, conducted through the tanks thus occupied, and brought into connection with all the various parts by a sufficiency of conducting wires and rods, decomposes the solution, liberates the silver from the other component elements, and deposits it in a beautifully clear and equable layer on the articles hanging in the tank. By increasing or decreasing these four agents—the intensity of the galvanic current, the quantity of the current, the strength of the solution, and the time of immersion—any desired thickness of silver may be deposited : the determination of all these points being a matter of experience on the part of those employed. As, from the peculiar nature of the process, the quantity of silver deposited cannot be ascertained while the deposition is going on, it is determined by weighing the article accurately before immersing it in the solution, and after it is finished; the former weight subtracted from the latter, gives the weight of silver deposited. If the solution be acted on for a long time together, it would become exhausted of its silver, and the process would stop for want of working materials; to obviate which, sheets of pure silver are suspended in the tanks at intervals, and the silver from these sheets becomes dissolved as fast as deposition takes place; so that the solution is constantly receiving on the one hand an equivalent for what it is giving up on the other. These sheets of silver are gradually eaten away, until they present nothing but a delicate web of lace-like fibres, extremely beautiful in appearance.

By changes in the ingredients used, and in the mode of proceeding, articles are coated with gold instead of silver. Many highly finished articles present a silver exterior, with a gilt interior. This is effected by the electro-process thus: the article is first silvered in the way just described; and the surface is then coated with some protective composition which will resist the deposition of gold. The article is next transferred to another vessel, where a film of gold is deposited on the side or surface required, without attacking the opposite side. This principle is carried still further, in some kinds of ornamental plate, by interspersing gold amongst the silver in very tasteful array; the silver in every such case, being protected from the subsequent action of the gold at every place where the latter metal is not required to be deposited. As the plated articles have a dead appearance when removed from the solution, they are rubbed with "scratch brushes," and then burnished, whereby a surface of great brilliancy is produced. Messrs. Elkington and Co., of Birmingham, exhibit some magnificent specimens of electro-plating.

Magnetism is now employed as a substitute for the galvanic battery in the various processes of electro-gilding, plating, &c. Independently of economy, the magnetic machine possesses the great advantages of uniformity of action, and of being devoid of all annoyances from any gaseous fumes, such as are always evolved from the voltaic battery.

The solutions from which gold and silver are generally precipitated, either by the voltaic or magnetic process, are those of the cyanide or sulphite of those metals : these salts being more employed than any others. Electro-platers give a preference, particularly for silver, to the solution of sulphite, as not being liable to spontaneous decomposition, as being unaccompained by any unpleasant smell, and yielding silver of considerable hardness and very white.

MANUFACTURE OF STEEL AND CUTLERY.

Fabrication de l'Acier et de Coutellerie.
Stahl und Stahlwaaren Manufactur.

THE bar-iron, produced as described at p. 23, is now ready to undergo that peculiar modification, which gives to it the name of steel. For this purpose, bars of iron are placed in what are termed converting furnaces, between layers of coarsely powdered charcoal, and submitted to the action of intense heat for many days, carbon is absorbed, and the iron converted into steel.

According to the various purposes for which steel is required, a lower or higher degree of conversion is employed; for instance, steel for coach-springs, is exposed to a lower heat than any other kind ; steel for knife-blades, and other purposes, requires a higher conversion ; steel for files, a yet higher degree ; and steel, which is afterwards to be cast in a fluid state, the highest of all. In the state in which it is obtained from the converting furnace it is called *blister* steel ; the name *common steel*, is given to it, when, after having been again heated, it is hammered with a very ponderous hammer, whereby a tougher quality is imparted to it. The name *shear steel* is given to it when it has undergone a process somewhat analogous to the welding of iron. It consists in heating several pieces to a white heat, and hammering them one upon another until all form one mass, far more dense, compact, and tough than the blister steel, from which it was made. This operation is performed in the *tilt* or *shear-house*. The term shear steel, is given to this kind of steel because it was found suitable to the manufacture of shears. It may be frequently seen stamped on table-knives. When closel examined, shear steel is found to have lost all the flaws and blisters which distinguished it as bliste steel, to have acquired a uniformity of character throughout, and to be greatly more malleable and tenacious than it was before. The beauty of modern steel goods is chiefly indebted to another kind of steel, termed *cast steel;* for this purpose, the steel is melted in a crucible, capable of containing 35 lbs., (for which purpose a most intense heat is required), when it is run into moulds, forming ingots of cast steel. All steel for the best articles, whether shear or cast, undergoes the process of tilting, before being applied to use. The object being to close the pores of the steel, and to render it as dense and compact as possible. The tilting process consists in heating the bars of steel to a certain heat, and submitting them to the action of a powerful tilt hammer. Notwithstanding the immensity of our iron manufacture, all our finest steel is made from Swedish iron: that from the Dannemora mine being preferred. The cause of the superiority of the Swedish iron, has never yet been explained; some chemists ascribe it to the presence of manganese, some to the presence of silica, while others suppose it to arise from the nature of the process employed. Various attempts have been made to imitate the steel made from Swedish iron, by the addition of preparations of manganese to English iron.

Sheffield is the metropolis of the manufacture of steel, and the various articles of steel manufactured therefrom. The average annual quantity of steel produced in Sheffield, during the last five years, is from 16,000 to 17,000 tons from foreign iron, and from 1,500 to 2,000 tons of British iron. The coal found in the neighbourhood of Sheffield, is what is termed a pure *hot* coal, free from earthy particles, and is, on that account, the best coal for converting iron into steel, in which process it is requisite to be able to obtain both a high and even temperature: and as it makes little or no deposit on the bars, it does not interrupt the even course of the draught. In 1835, there were but 36 steel converting furnaces in Sheffield, now there are upwards of 120. One furnace is computed to produce six tons of steel per week, requiring in the process six tons of converting coal. There are also upwards of 100 steel-melting furnaces, with 1,000 holes for crucibles; four tons of hard coke are required to make one ton of cast or melted steel; and ten holes produce four-and-a-half tons of steel per week. Upwards of 230,000 tons of coal are annually consumed in Sheffield in the manufacture of steel. In 1835, the quantity of unwrought steel exported was 2,810 tons, of which 1,886 tons were exported to the United States of America. In 1849, the total exported was 8,095 tons, of which 5,216 tons were sent to the United States. The quantity exported in 1850, was 10,587 tons, of the declared value of £393,659. In France, St. Etienne is the principal seat of the steel manufacture. Considerable progress has been made, but our continental rivals are still unable to compete with us in the manufacture of any kind of steel or iron, and if it were not for the high protecting duties, the French steel trade could not exist. In the Duchy of De Berg, in Prussia, there is a large manufactory of steel. Considerable mines of iron exist in the neighbourhood, but the quality of the iron is inferior to that obtained from Siegen, in Styria, and Eusdorf, in Bavaria. The steel manufacturers of De Berg, consequently purchase iron from those places, and mix it with their own metal to great advantage.

SCISSOR MANUFACTURE.

The scissor trade is one of the oldest of the staple trades of Sheffield, and requires very skilful and ingenious workmen, more so than any other branch of the cutlery manufacture. This trade is divided into twelve or fourteen stages, the principal of which are forging the scissors from a rod of steel of a suitable size, filing or ornamenting the shanks and bows, grinding and putting together, which includes screw-making, setting, or making the scissors work evenly together, and whetting. The forging branch is the most difficult to learn, requiring from six to seven years' practice to forge the ordinary kinds of scissors with precision. The total number of workmen and women employed in the trade is from 800 to 1,000, of which number, 130 are forgers, who will make, on the average, from sixteen to eighteen dozens per week. Messrs. Wilkinson and Son, the eminent scissor manufacturers of Sheffield, exhibit a series of specimens illustrating the process of manufacture, from the steel to the finished scissor; also a splendid pair of scissors cut out of solid steel, a duplicate of which Messrs. Wilkinson and Son had the honour of presenting to Her Majesty.

KNIFE MANUFACTURE.

In the manufacture of table knives and forks, it is usual to construct the better kinds with balance handles, thereby rendering it necessary to extend the hole beyond the length of the tang (the part inserted in the handle); it is also necessary that the perforation should be of larger dimensions than is absolutely necessary for the tang itself, in order to afford room for the introduction of lead, or some other heavy body; the bore also requires to be of large dimensions, for the introduction of the composition by which the blade is retained. From these causes, the handles of knives and forks are subject to considerable injury, the heat to which they are subjected being liable to crack and split them. This is especially the case in the smaller descriptions of table knives and forks, in which the handle is short, thereby requiring the bore to be large, by which means the substance of the handle is rendered very light. The blades of knives and forks, secured in the ordinary way, become loose and drop out. Messrs. Burdekins and Greening, in the manufacture of their improved knives and forks, form the hole in the handle of the exact size required for the introduction of the tang, which passes nearly through, and of such weight, together with the handle, as to balance the blade, the extreme end being secured by a screw cut on the tang, having a cap nut, which is furnished with a shoulder, butting against a shoulder recess at that end of the handle. The screw being firmly set, will retain the handle in its position on the tang; it may also be readily undone, whenever it may be required to renew the blade, as handles constructed on this principle, if of agate or ivory, are more lasting than the blades, which may thus be renewed as required; the handles themselves sustaining little wear, and, by reason of their increased strength, from the smallness of the bore, not being liable to fracture. In some cases, the handle is connected with the tang by means of a ferrule, in which case the ferrule is placed partly on the shoulder of the blade, and partly on the handle, by which means the junction of the two is more effectually secured.

PEN AND POCKET KNIFE MANUFACTURE.

This important branch of the cutlery trade of Sheffield, employs a larger number of hands than any other. The workmen are divided into three classes, viz.: the *blade forgers*, who, out of a rod of steel, form the blade of the knife by hammering, and afterwards harden it by immersion whilst hot in cold water; the *scale and spring forgers*, who form the inner metallic scale in which the blade lies when shut, and the spring or piece of steel, which, running along the back edge of the knife, separates the two scales or halves of the handle, and by its elasticity exerted upon the tang of the blade, secures it in any required position; and the *hafter*, who forms the ivory or pearl outer scales of the handle. To these must be added the makers of other smaller parts, and the workman whose office it is to build up the knife out of the materials ready to his hand.

The superior kinds of surgical instruments, such as lancets, dissecting and operating knives, are also manufactured at Sheffield. In this branch of the cutlery trade, Messrs. Hutchinsons, of Norfolk-street, deservedly occupy the foremost place, and their cutting instruments and general surgical implements, find their way into most of the hospitals of our own and foreign countries.

RAZOR MANUFACTURE.

There is, perhaps, no branch of the cutlery trade, which has excited more attention—on which more has been written—or in the preparation of which more care is taken—than the razor manufacture; the good quality requisite to the fit action of a razor, having made it an object of moment both to the steel maker and the cutler. The quality of the steel employed, and the grinding and tempering of the blade, are all important points in the manufacture of a razor intended not merely "for sale," but "for use." Messrs. Rodgers, Mr. George Wolstenholme, and other celebrated Sheffield cutlers exhibit some fine specimens of razors, the manufacture of which is carried to so high a degree of perfection in the "metropolis of steel."

SWORD MANUFACTURE.

The steel is brought to the form of what are called *sword-moulds*, either at Sheffield or at Birmingham, these sword-moulds being bars fitted in size and shape for swords. The bars are heated and are forged into shape by two men, the 'maker' and the 'striker,' much in the same way as cutlery. When the sword is required to be hollowed at the surfaces, it is hammered between steel bosses or swages. Then ensue the processes of hardening and tempering, on which so much of the excellence of the sword depends, the hardening being effected by a sudden cooling after heating, and the tempering by a gradual cooling. As the blade has become somewhat distorted in form by these processes, it is twisted straight and regular by confining it at certain points, and forcibly bending it in the proper direction. The whole surface is then ground upon a large stone, and an edge given to it. As it loses some of its temper by this process, it is again tempered and afterwards polished. The making of the handles is a separate department of the manufacture, depending for its character on the costliness of the materials employed.

An important stage in the manufacture of every sword is the 'proof' to which it is subjected, a proof consisting of a series of tests much more violent than the sword is likely ever to undergo.

Although Sheffield is the head-quarter of the cutlery trade generally, Birmingham has always been the chief seat of the sword manufacture.

The cutlery of Sheffield is known all over the world, and it is not a little curious to see knives and other articles fabricated there for the use of far distant lands, so peculiar in their form, and so peculiarly adapted to uses with which we are not at all familiar, that the traveller in Russia or South America, might readily be excused, for bringing over some "peculiar" article of native use as a "curiosity" to his friends at home, which had originally been made at Sheffield.

The visitor will not fail to observe the extensive assortment and great variety of articles of cutlery, suited for every market, manufactured and exhibited by Messrs. Unwin and Rodgers. The traveller to distant lands, or the intending emigrant, will here be reminded of his probable require-ments in this department of "outfitting," by the sight of daggers, dirks, American, Indian hunting, and bowie knives. The Californian gold seeker will find knives especially constructed for self-defence; the sailor, the

sportsman, the gardener, the farmer, and every class of society will each meet with a variety of the peculiar kind of knife best adapted to his pur-pose; while the ingenious combination of several useful articles in one, not merely for show, but for actual use, will deservedly merit the attention of every visitor. The price varies, and shows a greater variety than the pattern itself, and few would believe it possible to make a knife with a wrought steel blade for three farthings each, when, at the same time, the price may be increased by superior workmanship and ornament, to £1 each, or to any price required, and each retain its correct value. But when it is stated that the knives sold for three farthings, and one penny each, are the combined workmanship of at least six branches of the trade, the possibility may be doubted by one unacquainted with the art. Besides all kinds of knives, Messrs. Unwin and Rodgers manufacture razors of the finest to the

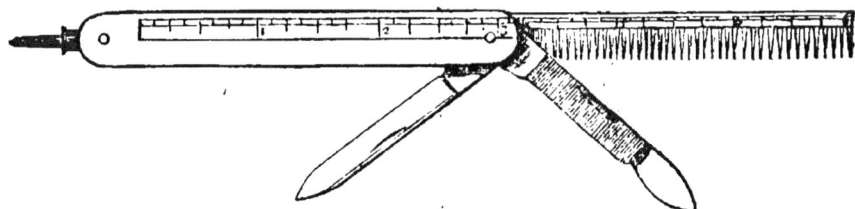

commonest quality, nail-files, button-hooks, and all kinds of fancy articles for ladies' companions and gentlemen's dressing-cases. They are also the inventors and patentees of several exceedingly useful and convenient articles, one of which, the " Patent Pencil-knife," contains a superior ever-pointed pencil, with a reserve for leads, a silver tooth-pick, and two good pen blades, the whole handsomely put together, with German silver mountings.

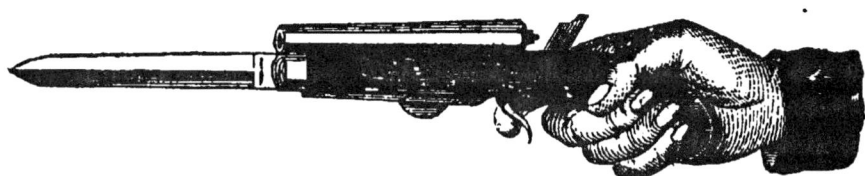

Another, which may be called the pencil-comb measure-knife, contains, in addition to the foregoing, a comb and six-inch rule, forming a complete *multum-in-parvo*. Many of our readers know, by experience, the great inconvenience of a waistcoat pocket literally crammed with sundry useful articles, each and all highly necessary to personal comfort and convenience, —such as a penknife, a pencil, a comb, a rule, a tooth-pick, &c. Messrs. Unwin and Rodgers seem especially to have succeeded in an ingenious contrivance to remedy this inconvenience; so that we may, by providing ourselves with one of these really admirable pocket companions, have only *one* article to seek for instead of five or six. To another form of pencil-knife, with penholder, Messrs. U. & R. have lately registered an addition, which, to many gentlemen, will prove no slight recommendation,—it is a *cigar-holder*, a neat little contrivance, which in no way interferes with the use of the pencil or knife, and as it shuts into the handle, like a knife blade, it does not diminish its portability. Another useful instrument is called the "improved far west American hunting knife and self protector," and a very formidable companion it is, as it contains, besides a penknife and hunting blade,—a pistol, accompanied with bullet, mould, ram-rod, picker, tweezer, and ammunition-box, with caps and balls, all complete and ready for use.

FILES, EDGE TOOLS, &c.

The manufacture of files, saws, and edge-tools, forms other important branches of the trade of Sheffield. These articles are exported to all parts of the globe, and there is scarcely a corner of the wide world, where a British ship is allowed to enter, but could exhibit some specimens of Sheffield steel goods. The great majority of visitors to the Exhibition will probably devote but little attention to the specimens of Sheffield files exhibited. Files, however, are the working tools by which every other kind of working tools is, in some degree, fashioned, and are, therefore, amongst the most important articles in the work-shop of the artizan. Whether a man is making a watch or a steam-engine, a knife or a plough, a pin or a coach, he can make no progress without the assistance of this useful tool. The whole of the files manufactured are still made by hand, notwithstanding the various ingenious machines which have been contrived to supersede manual labour, in this department of the Sheffield trade. The workmen in the file trade are divided into four classes, viz., the *forger*, who heats the steel and hammers the file into shape, and is responsible for its quality; the *grinder*, who grinds the "blank" files to a true and regular surface; the *cutter*, who makes the necessary indentations or grooves on the blank file; and the *hardener*, who tempers the file when made. The files are then cleaned by women, and each carefully tested by a superior foreman.

SAW MANUFACTURE.

This trade is divided into three branches, viz., saw making, saw-handle making, and saw grinding, at all of which men and boys are employed. Women are employed to rub and scour the saws, and wrap them up. The common saws are made of sheet-iron; those of a better quality are made of shear-steel, and the best are formed of cast-steel. The sheets of metal having been cut of the required size and thickness, the teeth are each formed separately, by means of a punching-machine. The saw is then hardened and planished, whereby it is made true and of equal elasticity in every part; it is then ground; and lastly, the teeth are bent in alternate directions by hammering.

In the manufacture of edge-tools, the workmen are divided into three classes, viz., forgers, grinders, and hardeners; the first of whom prepares the tool, the second grinds it, and the third hardens it to the required temper. Some idea of the "grinding" trade of Sheffield, may be obtained from the fact, that one house, in the edge-tool trade, consumes 12,000 tons of grindstones per annum. Messrs W. and S. Butcher, who, we believe, are the largest manufacturers and exporters of edge-tools, files, and razors, in Sheffield, exhibit specimens of steel, edge-tools, files, saws, and razors, in which superior workmanship is combined with economy of price.

Messrs. Slack, Sellars, and Grayson, of Sheffield, manufacture an improved tenon saw, with tubular back; the increased stiffness afforded by this construction, preventing the saw from buckling, or being easily bent.

The value of hardwares and cutlery exported, in 1850, was £2,639,728, more than one-third of which was sent to the United States of America; British India and the Hanseatic towns also take large quantities.

In 1849, 6,003 cwts. of elephants' teeth or tusks, and 1,047 tons of horns and horn tips were consumed in this country, of which a large portion was used in the manufacture of handles for knives, cutting instruments, &c.

ETCHING AND GILDING ON STEEL.

Our readers will notice the beautiful designs on some of the steel articles, razors, &c., sent from Sheffield. The method of executing this etching and gilding on steel, is the invention of Mr. Thomas Skinner, of Sheffield. It is true that prior to Mr. Skinner's discovery, steel articles were etched and gilded: this however was accomplished by means of hand-tools, the expense and labour attending which, precluded the adoption of the process, except in goods of an expensive character. The leading features of Mr. Skinner's process, are its simplicity, clearness, and cheapness; any design occupying the space of a razor blade, no matter how much work it contains—for instance, twenty or thirty figures, a view of London, the ruins of an old abbey, or any other subject can be etched at the low price of one farthing, or less. Mr. Skinner's process is indeed a complete triumph over the old system of ornamenting steel, and it has opened up an entirely new field for the most beautiful designs the skill of the artist can furnish. The process is effected by transfer of a copper-plate engraving: and a large number of goods can be etched or gilded in a very short space of time. The blades of the razors exported to America, are often ornamented by this process: but we hear that in the home trade the process is not much adopted for this purpose: persons having an idea, that the ornament is added to conceal defects in the quality of the blade.

STEEL PENS.

The manufacture of steel pens next requires a passing observation. For producing them, the best Dannemora Swedish iron or hoop iron is selected. It is worked into sheets or slips about three feet long, and four or five inches broad; the thickness varying with the desired stiffness and flexibility of the pen for which it is intended. By a stamping press, pieces of the required size are cut out. The point intended for the nib is introduced into a gauged hole, and by a machine pressed into a semi-cylinrical shape; in the same machine it is pierced with the required slit or slits. This being effected, the pens are cleaned by mutual attrition in tin cylinders, and tempered by being brought to the required colour, by the application of heat. It unfortunately happens, however, that the process of tempering, upon which the quality of the pen entirely depends, is in most cases carelessly performed. Some idea of the extent of this manufacture will be formed from the statement, that nearly 150 tons of steel are employed annually for this purpose, producing upwards of 250,000,000 pens.

Mr. Gillott, of Birmingham, who manufactures 120,000,000 annually, is the principal exhibitor of steel pens.

STEEL PLATES.

Another branch of steel manufacture which, though limited in extent, is of great importance in the arts, is the manufacture of steel plates for engraving, which, notwithstanding all the attempts made from time to time, was not accomplished until 1810. To Mr. Perkins, of New England, and, subsequently, to Mr. Warren, and Mr. Hughes, we are indebted for the removal of the difficulties that so long stood in the way of preparing steel plates, by the successful application of which, to engraving, we may now obtain for a few pence, fine copies of the best works of the best masters, thus improving the taste and cultivating the love for the beautiful in art and nature. The process of manufacture consists in exposing the plate of steel to such a carefully regulated temperature, and slowly cooling it, that it becomes very ductile, and may be readily cut with the engraving tool. The steel plates manufactured and exhibited by Mr. Sellars, of Sheffield, are of very superior quality.

Although the season of the year may not recal· the healthy amusement of skating to the mind of the visitor; notwithstanding the Serpentine is so near, yet he will not fail to admire the "Royal Albert Skates," of which

Messrs. Marsden, Brothers, and Silverwood, of Sheffield, are the manufacturers. A pair of these handsome skates having been made by them for Prince Albert, and presented through Colonel C. B. Phipps, that gentleman wrote a letter in reply, intimating His Royal Highness's gracious acceptance of the same, and expressing also the Prince's admiration of the design and workmanship. The following is a description of these skates, one of which is shown in the accompanying engraving :—The irons represent a swan in the attitude of swimming, and are beautifully chased to form the

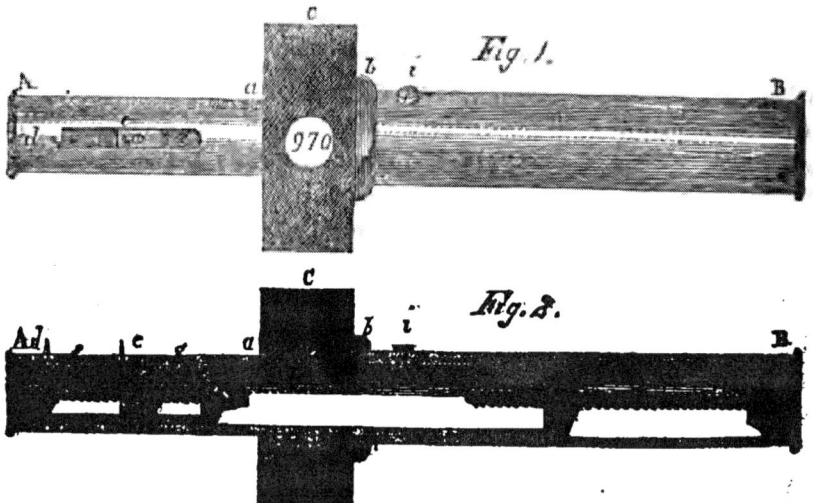

feathers : the wood being carved to correspond. Round the heel are carved the national emblems : the rose, shamrock, and thistle. In each skate are four strap-holes, lined with gold. On the part where the toe rests is a gold plate, having engraved upon it the makers' name and address. In the centre where the ball of the foot rests, is the " Royal Arms," studded with gold. On the heel a silver star is let into the wood, and surrounded by a golden garter, with the motto, " *Honi soit qui mal y pense*," engraved upon it, It is decidedly the handsomest skate ever produced.

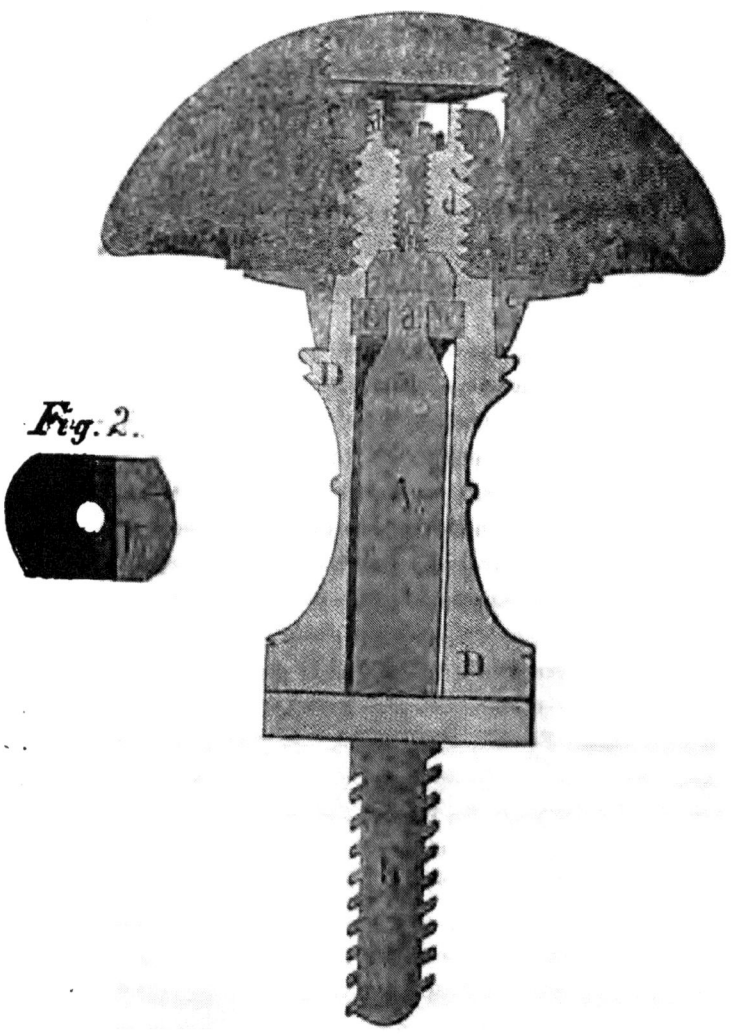

Messrs. Marsden, Brothers, and Silverwood, are the manufacturers also of some registered tools: of two of which the annexed engravings are a representation.   The first is their " Registered Brace Head," which will be found to possess that combination of advantages long sought for by artizans, viz., security of the head to the brace—ease in working—without friction—and ultimate durability ; and on these grounds this invention claims a preference before all others yet manufactured.

Improved Mortice-Guage.—Messrs. Marsden & Co. also exhibit their improved mortice-guage, an important aid to such workmen as value correctness with economy of time and labour. The important advantage it possesses over other guages, consists in its not being altered by accident when once fixed in the required position ; this is a great recommendation to the use of the registered mortice-guage, the ordinary guages being very liable to alteration, whereby the workman suffers serious inconvenience. We recommend these instruments to the artizan visitors.

ENCAUSTIC TILES.

ENCAUSTIC tiles are thus prepared :—A clay of good quality, but of a red or buff colour, is pressed into a mould, which gives the form to the tile, and leaves an impression 1-4th of an inch in depth, to be filled with variously-coloured clays. On leaving the mould, the tiles are allowed to harden in the air, after which the coloured material, composed of Devonshire or Cornish clay, and some metallic oxides, is then poured over the whole surface in a state of thick slip, when it is again dried to a certain extent. A layer of fine clay is also applied to the back of the tile, which is pierced with holes in the first process of moulding ; as the finer clay does not contract so much in firing as the common kind, of which the body is made, those holes serve to seal the two varieties of clay together, and to equalize the contraction of the mass. The attention which has been given by Messrs. Minton and Co., to this branch of manufacture, and the amount of skill and scientific knowledge displayed in the improvement of all the processes connected with the production of this class of artificial stone, cannot be too highly commended. As an ornamental paving for the halls of houses, or any open spaces in public buildings, nothing can be more beautiful ; and from its extreme durability, it is really economical. There is evidently a growing taste for this species of decoration, and since, by the aids of modern science, we are not only enabled to execute all that the ancients did, but to employ many colours with which they were not acquainted ; we can produce finer specimens of the Mosaic art than any which have been preserved from the ravages of Vandalism, or the decaying touch of time.

PRINTING IN OIL COLOURS.

Mr. George Baxter, the patentee of the process of printing in oil colours, exhibits in the Fine Art Court, upwards of sixty specimens (from the largest size to the smallest miniature), of his choicest productions, most tastefully arranged in a handsome frame, glazed with plate glass. The visitors will indeed be delighted with these charming specimens which form the principal attraction in the Fine Art Court. Baxter's oil colour paintings, are now as well known, (and perhaps are more appreciated) in every town on the continent as in England; and the printers and engravers there, are puzzled how the prints can be executed and sold at so low a price. The great secret of this is, the immense demand which has arisen for these beautiful productions; thousands daily are printed, and yet the patentee finds it a difficult matter to keep the public supplied with them. More than fifteen years have now elapsed since Mr. Baxter patented his original process, during which time, he has gone on steadily and perseveringly improving his process, which has now attained perfection. Many difficulties occurred in the earlier stages, but the energy and preseverance of Mr. Baxter, succeeded in surmounting them. Upwards of £8,000 had been expended by him in his experiments, before renumerative returns were obtained by Mr. Baxter, and just as he had succeeded in bringing the process to perfection, the time of his patent right expired. It was therefore an act of justice on the part of the Judicial Committee of the Privy Council, to grant Mr. Baxter an extension of five years from the date of the expiration of his patent, in order to afford him time to secure to himself the pecuniary reward for his labours, which he has so well deserved. Mr. Baxter's perseverance in bringing his work to the degree of perfection it has obtained, deserves such a mark of commendation; and his just claims in the discovery, and continued improvement of this process, equally deserves the fullest protection and encouragement, which the present patent laws can afford. The *Art Journal* speaking of Baxter's procees of printing in oil colours says, " to show the simplicity of the patent process, we may here remark that nearly the whole is worked by boys, the most chaste and delicate colours being produced by their labour; and though, as in all novelties, difficulties at first abounded, by energy and preseverance, Mr. Baxter succeeded in surmounting them.

The general encouragement given to the new art is beyond precedent, several of the pictures produced by the patent process having reached the enormous sale of 300,000 copies. By these striking results many branches of trade have been greatly benefited, numerous hands have been employed, and the public supplied with specimens of art of sterling merit. It may be hoped, therefore, that the circulation of these pictures, elaborate and beautiful in their character, may supersede the tasteless daubs we too frequently find even in the drawing-room, and so constantly in the cottage; and that thus the tastes of the people may be cultivated, and the minds of all classes refined. For beautiful as are these productions, they may be purchased at so low a rate as to be within the means of the working classes; indeed their wonderful cheapness has rendered them useful for a variety of purposes never contemplated by the patentee when he turned his attention to the production of coloured pictures."

The visitor will notice in the Fine Art Court, a variety of specimens of lithographic printing by Hanhart, Kronheim, &c., but the productions of lithographers will not stand comparison with Baxter's exquisite engravings. Hanhart's colour printing is very good, and carried to a certain degree of perfection, but there are many difficulties attendant on this process, such as the matter, &c., which materially interferes with its successful application. The same observations apply to Kronheim's specimens, undoubtedly good as productions of lithography. In the specimen of the crucifixion exhibited, there is a great want of variety in the tints and roundings which is entirely lost, and it has too much of the appearance of a stiff dark print, after the style of a juvenile artist. We very much doubt the wisdom of these attempts at coloured lithographs, when such productions can be obtained by the wood block process of Baxter, especially as we understand that nearly 50 drawings on stone are required for the completion of such a lithograph as that exhibited, not more than thirty or forty of which can be executed in a week. Baxter's process on the contrary, is one for the million, thousands being daily produced.

By placing elaborate and beautiful paintings, such as these, within the means of the industrial classes, the taste of the community cannot fail to be improved.

The best specimens of lithographic printing are those executed by Mr. Owen Jones, whose name has obtained so much celebrity of late in connection with the decoration of the building; his productions in lithography are unsurpassed; yet even these yield the palm to Baxter's oil colours.

Rowney's water colour engravings, erroneously so termed, are merely specimens of block printing by the ordinary process employed by the ornamental printers, the same process as the lottery bills; the effect produced is but inferior. The Fine Art Court contains some very beautiful specimens of carving in oak, ornamental marbles, models in wax, ivory, cork, architectural models, &c.

DAGUERREOTYPE PORTRAITS, &c.

Portraits &c. Daguerreotypes.   Daguerreotyp Portraits, &c.

———

When we were first made acquainted with the development of the photographic power, and witnessed the production of a miniature portrait by the simple agency of light acting upon a metallic surface, we were certainly astonished at the result, though we must admit those pictures gave us no heartfelt gratification.

Warmth and life were wanting in features, "so coldly sweet, so deadly air." The absence of relief and roundness of form contributed also to increase our distaste for likenesses taken by the Daguerreotype. We considered, however, that a great step was made in the discovery of an art, which time and research might eventually perfect. The portraits obtained by Mr. Beard's new process, have much delighted us; he has brought his chemical and scientific knowledge to bear so well on the subject as to give colour and contour to the leaden and flat surface. The figure stands out boldly from the background; and a picture is speedily produced, very far superior to any that had been obtained by former experiments.

We would especially notice the admirable effect of the flesh tints; which appear as if actually embodied in the miniature, and not, as we generally see them, spread on the surface.

The more recent improvements effected in this branch of the Fine Arts, are very great. They consist in imparting a greater degree of softness to the picture, and in fixing the whole by a chemical process, resulting in the formation of a transparent enamel, which is inalterable, and effectually preserves the brightest and most delicate colours from the action of light, air, and water, rendering a glass covering quite unnecessary.

In addition to the well known application of the Daguerreotype to landscapes, buildings, &c., Mr. Beard has successfully applied it to obtaining copies of machinery, reduced to any scale required, ready for the use of the engraver and lithographer. A few moments thus suffice to take the most correct and accurate representation of a complicated machine, the details of which would require an artist several days to master.

MACHINERY.

In the department of machinery, on the north side of the buildings, the attention of the visitor will be struck with the great excellence of the various contributions. Amongst these we would more especially mention Donnesthorpe's patent machine, for opening cotton wool, a quarter of the right, in which he has disposed of, it is said for £25,000; Mather's machine for printing calico in eight colours; Garforth's new riveting machine; and Hick and Sons hydraulic press pump, by means of which, with its four cylinders instead of one, an enormous pressure is obtained. Maudesley exhibits his ingenious machine for coining medals, which substitutes the use of a cam instead of a screw, and gives a result, obtained by increased leverage, instead of one obtained by increased momentum. Mr. Appold's centrifugal pump forms a very attractive object: by it the inventor calculates that, with a wheel 20 feet diameter, describing 53½ revolutions per minute, he would discharge in that short time 560,000 gallons of water. In addition to the tools exhibited by Whitworth, of Manchester, is a machine, which can be ascertained by the touch, to measure the 250,000ths part of an inch, and which, it is believed, may be made to measure *the millionth part of an inch*. Nasmyth's hammer, the morticing and tenon machines of Furness, the beautiful hand-printing machines of Applegath, and the ingeniously constructed corn-mill of Westrup, will excite attention. The locomotive department is well furnished; the monster engine of the North Western Railway Company, and Stephenson's engine, constructed on Crampton's patent, are here conspicuous. In the section of fixed machinery, the visitor will notice the splendid marine engines of Bolton and Watts, and of Penn, remarkable for their economy of space, their direct action, and the finished workmanship they display.

The annexed engraving, which we received too late to place with the account given of it at p. 62, to which we refer the reader, represents Fourdrinier's Patent Safety Apparatus, in use. The rope is here shown as broken, and the cage and its contents, instead of being precipitated to the bottom of the coal-pit, is firmly secured to the sides of the pit, and the miner thus rescued from impending destruction.

DRY GAS METER.

Of Defries' Dry Gas Meter, nothing more need be said, than that there are upwards of 40,000 of them in use, in various public buildings and private houses throughout the empire, the continent, and the colonies; whilst at the Thames Tunnel two large meters have been in constant use, night and day, for five years, being equal to forty years of ordinary use. The meter constructed by Mr. Defries for the new House of Commons, is calculated to pass 10,000 feet of gas per hour, and to supply 2,000 lights, and has been pronounced by many eminent gas engineers of the day, to be the most magnificent measuring machine ever constructed by human hands.

Of the various uses to which gas has been hitherto applied, none exceeds its employment for heating the water of a bath. By means of Mr. Defries' recently patented improvements, the temperature of 45 gallons of water can be raised from 50° to 95° Fah. in five or six minutes, and that too at the small cost of less than twopence.

Mr. Defries has also constructed a gas-cooking apparatus, forming an invaluable domestic agent, by means of which the varied operations of boiling, baking, stewing, broiling, roasting, and straining, may be carried on at one and the same moment; in which economy, cleanliness, uniform heat, the preservation of the juices of the meat, are combined with the great advantages of the apparatus being always ready for use at a moment's notice.

Since writing the article on Woollen Manufacture, we regret to find that after incurring considerable outlay in preparation for the Exhibition, Messrs. Nicoll felt themselves compelled to withdraw their names from the list of exhibitors. For the specimens intended to be exhibited, we must therefore refer our readers to 114, Regent-street.

Erratum.—Page 70, for 133,000 read 238,000; for 23,000 read 100,000; and for 110,000 read 123,000. After *twelve months*, add "and most of the remainder were little inferior."

CONTENTS.

CONTENTS.

Printed at the "Patent Journal" Printing Office, 89, Chancery Lane, London.

Lightning Source UK Ltd.
Milton Keynes UK
20 June 2010

155893UK00004B/20/P